THE WALL STREET JOURNAL.

NATIONAL BUSINESS EMPLOYMENT WEEKLY

Premier Guides

WEEKLY

NETWORKING

THE NATIONAL BUSINESS EMPLOYMENT WEEKLY PREMIER GUIDES SERIES

Published:

Resumes, ISBN# 0-471-31029-8 cloth;
ISBN# 0-471-31028-X paper

Interviewing, ISBN# 0-471-31024-7 cloth;
ISBN# 0-471-31025-5 paper

Networking, ISBN# 0-471-31026-3 cloth;
ISBN# 0-471-31027-1 paper

Forthcoming:

Cover Letters, ISBN# 0-471-10671-2 cloth;
ISBN# 0-471-10672-0 paper

Alternative Careers, ISBN# 0-471-10919-3 cloth;
ISBN# 0-471-10918-5 paper

THE WALL STREET JOURNAL.

NATIONAL BUSINESS EMPLOYMENT WEEKLY

Premier Guides

NETWORKING

Douglas B. Richardson

John Wiley & Sons, Inc.
New York • Chichester • Brisbane • Toronto • Singapore

Author's Note on Usage

Throughout this book, the singular masculine pronoun ("he") is used to refer to job seekers of either gender. The sole intention is to avoid the awkwardness of "he and she" constructions, not to disparage either men or women.

The use of a noun, in this case *network,* as a verb is sometimes frowned upon. However, since *to network* has won acceptance in common parlance and is both convenient and clear, it is used freely in this book.

Library of Congress Cataloging in Publication Data:

National Business Employment Weekly.
    Networking / by National Business Employment Weekly.
      p.   cm.
    Includes bibliographical references.
    ISBN 0-471-31026-3 (cloth: alk. paper).—ISBN 0-471-31027-1 (pbk. : alk. paper)
    1. Job hunting. 2. Career changes. 3. Social networks.
I. Title.
HF5382.7.R53   1994
650.14—dc20   93-49881

Printed in the United States of America

10 9 8 7 6 5 4 3 2 1

Foreword

Trying to find a better job by calling people you don't know and asking them for help probably sounds dreadful, like a cross between telemarketing and door-to-door sales. After all, nobody likes rejection, and this approach is sure to provoke a rash of apologies and unreturned phone calls.

But what if it works? What if you can find a great new job (or project, if you're a consultant) simply by meeting with acquaintances and strangers who agree to see you? Would you try it?

The premise behind networking—the practice of contacting everyone you know (and everyone they know) to ask for advice and support—is that *it does work*.

A recent survey of more than 1,500 successful job hunters showed that 61 percent found new positions by tapping their networks of friends, family members, acquaintances and others willing to help. In comparison, 18 percent found jobs by answering ads and only 2 percent by sending unsolicited resumes to company recruiters, according to Drake Beam Morin Inc., a New York-based career consulting firm. The percentage of successful networkers is higher in towns and industries where everyone seems to know everyone else.

The key to networking is learning how to approach others without triggering their "nuisance" alarm. Doug Richardson's approach is effective because he understands the process thoroughly (including the potential negatives) and has counseled hundreds of job hunters on the strategies that work best for their specific situations.

In this well-researched, finely written book that's full of relevant anecdotes and case studies, Doug explains why an effective networking relationship helps both parties. Contacts typically enjoy talking about themselves, and if they can match you with a position somewhere, they're doing you a favor they hope will be returned one day. That's why networking is the business world's best example of a win–win relationship.

TONY LEE
Editor
National Business Employment Weekly

Acknowledgments

This book would not have happened without the support of Betsy, Kate and Holly, who provide my motivational gas, the vision of VJ Pappas, who, as an earlier editor of the *National Business Employment Weekly,* turned the ignition key and provided skilled initial driver education, and the continuing support of Tony Lee, present editor of *NBEW,* who keeps my pedal to the metal. Thanks also to Tom Cheney for the use of his witty cartoons.

This book is dedicated to everyone with whom I've ever networked, everyone who has ever networked with me, and the hundreds of clients over the years whose networking adventures have provided invaluable war stories, horror stories, cautionary tales, disasters and triumphs. They all are in here somewhere, proving the fundamental axiom that "Whatever goes around, comes around. You never know *when* it will come around, but if you don't go around, *nothing* will ever come around."

About the Author

Douglas B. Richardson is president of Richardson & Co., a career counseling and management development consulting firm in Bala Cynwyd, Pa. His previous positions include senior vice president with Manchester Inc., one of the nation's largest outplacement firms, and senior vice president with a regional executive search and management consulting firm. His early career included law practice as a litigator with Dechert, Price & Rhoads in Philadelphia, and as a federal and state prosecutor. He later was regional counsel for the Pennsylvania Department of Public Welfare before being named that agency's director of communications and press secretary.

Mr. Richardson earned a J.D. degree from Harvard Law School, an M.A. degree in communications from the University of Pennsylvania's Annenberg School and a B.A. from the University of Michigan's Honors College. He has been an adjunct professor at Temple and Drexel Universities, and lectures frequently for such organizations as the Wharton School, the Wharton Entrepreneurial Center and the Harvard Business School Association. Since 1984, he's been an award-winning *National Business Employment Weekly* columnist, as well as a frequent contributor to numerous other business and legal publications.

Contents

3 Who Should I See and Why Will They See Me?   51

4 Into the Fray: Asking for Meetings   67

5 What Goes On in a Networking Meeting   85

6 Where Good Vibes Come From   109

7 Scenarios and Situations: Voices from the Front   137

8 Looping Back and Following Up   155

9 Planning, Logistics and Keeping Track   165

10 Alternative Approaches and Techniques   175

11 What the Future Holds   189

Index   195

Introduction

The Technique Job Seekers Love to Hate

This book almost failed to see the light of day.

Some publishers wondered whether there was enough theory to networking to justify a whole book on the subject. Others questioned whether networking was just a fad, well on its way to becoming a cliché. Even some job seekers complained that networking successfully could be intensely frustrating, while potential employers occasionally labeled it a devious, much-abused pretext for outflanking their defenses and hitting them up for a job.

The editors of the *National Business Employment Weekly* (NBEW) stood their ground. Since 1981, this Dow Jones publication has been advising candidates on job-market trends, as well as on tips and techniques for becoming former job seekers. In those years, NBEW has learned something: whatever networking is, it works. Despite being abused, maligned or misunderstood, networking has proven to be the most productive technique for getting job market exposure, unearthing opportunities and landing employment. Year in and year out, about 60 percent of all positions are filled as a consequence of an informal, interpersonal contact, according to national surveys by such groups as the Association of Outplacement Consulting Firms and the American Management Association.

The *National Business Employment Weekly* continues to champion networking and, in its editors' view, a series of books bearing the NBEW's name could hardly fail to include a volume on the subject.

Actually, both sides are right. When carried out in a structured, systematic way, networking is a supereffective method of getting job market exposure and gathering useful information. On the other hand, there's no denying these facts:

1. The information gathered by networking is informal, anecdotal, potentially biased and frequently distorted or incomplete.

2. The world of gossip is completely disorganized and unpredictable. Months of networking activity may produce little useful information; then a snatch of conversation overheard at an airport may lead directly to the job of a lifetime.

The fundamental principle behind successful networking is familiar: What goes around comes around. The corollary states that a lot of going around may happen before anything comes around. Even more frustrating is the fact that no advance notice tells when job leads are going to come around. A meeting that seemed a total waste of time in August may produce an excited phone call in November: "I just heard of an opportunity that immediately made me think of you . . . ."

This book won't advance the proposition that networking is enjoyable. (Those who find networking a lot of fun and a real mind-expander should expect the scorn optimists always encounter.) Even skilled networkers often find the process stressful. And networking certainly isn't a science, or even an innovative approach to the age-old task of finding meaningful employment.

Networking is about human nature in action, and we all know that human nature is subjective, irrational and frequently unfair. In other words, it's a long way from the rationality and objectivity of science. There's no claim of discovery here; we're talking about an approach to securing employment that existed long before anyone chose to make a pop phenomenon out of it by hanging the "networking" label around its neck. People have been banging on their relatives, friends and acquaintances for help in finding work since Og was thrown out of the mastodon-hauling business by the invention of the wheel.

This book is simply a cookbook, a user's guide to a self-marketing approach that, frankly, most job seekers don't do very well. The main purpose of the following pages is to be practical—to give straight talk in plain English: who, what, where, why, when, how. As we dissect the whys and wherefores of networking, we'll periodically poke fun at it to keep ourselves from becoming pompous and unduly serious.

Networking needn't be made into more than it is. We can laugh at its excesses, twist it, fold it or make a funny party hat out of it; it will still outstrip any other job search technique. There's nothing magic about the word *networking*. If a little irreverence will make you feel more comfortable, frame the word in oral "quotation marks" whenever you utter it: "Joe? This is Doug. I wonder if we might arrange to get together for one of these . . . ah . . . 'networking' meetings." If the conversation is face-to-face, you can add little quotation-mark gestures in the air with your hands. Try it; it drives the phobia away.

Who Should Use This Book?

Every job seeker. This book is written primarily for them, although the ideas and techniques described herein will work equally well for developing "information power" once you land your new job. In fact, everyone at every level in the working world, whether looking for work or not and whether realizing it or not, is constantly networking as a way of staying on top of things and creating useful connections.

Anyone running a "conventional" job search—that is, looking for a job that's a logical extension of a prior career—will find plenty of networking advice here. A variety of techniques can be used in addition to networking: answering ads, trying to catch the attention of recruiters and headhunters, and trying to make "direct contact" with potential employers, usually by sending a cover letter with a resume attached. However, most pie charts depicting the relative effectiveness of job search techniques say that ads fill no more than about 20 percent of all openings. Recruiters, headhunters and other "broker" types probably fill half that amount, and no more than 5 percent are filled via mass mailings, "targeted letters" and other forms of direct contact.

About two-thirds of all "conventional" jobs get filled, according to the U.S. Department of Labor, in "informal" ways—through gossip, word-of-mouth, relatives, friends, acquaintances and behind-the-scenes favors. The methods that people use to tap into this wellspring of information and create job market exposure for themselves are not new. In recent years, the word *networking* has come into fashion to describe them.

For anyone making a major change in career direction or emphasis, the ability to build and draw on informal interpersonal networks is absolutely essential. None of the other conventional job search techniques—ads, headhunters or direct contact—works very well for career changers. Ads slot conventionally credentialed people into conventionally defined roles; career changers represent a risk most employers are hesitant to take. This is doubly true with headhunters, who collect large fees to reduce employers' hiring risks. Headhunters don't take chances on untried, untested possibilities. They avoid career changers like the plague.

Direct contact doesn't work much better for career changers than for anyone else. The inescapable conclusion is that networking is the only job search technique that works for people who are making a major shift in job role or setting.

Networking ability is crucial:

☆ For consultants starting new practices.

☆ For entrepreneurs looking for financial angels, coventurers or qualified colleagues.

☆ For anyone marketing ideas, programs or concepts.

☆ For anyone operating in the political arena (lobbying is no more than licensed networking).

☆ For anyone in a setting where whom you know is as important as what you know.

Are you one of those people who think that cultivating "connections" is somehow illicit or sleazy, that all of life's activities should be conducted on pure merit and that networking is a technique for creating privilege or unfair advantage? Are you uncomfortable about "trying to work the angles"? Networking isn't about angles; it's about creating access to opportunity. You can't win if you don't play, and you can't play if you don't know where the game is.

Throughout this book, we'll be talking about techniques, not about manipulation, deception or selling someone a false bill of goods. We'll work on the most effective ways to build rapport and trust and to present an undistorted picture of your strengths and virtues. In focusing on predictable patterns of human nature, our purpose is to communicate *you,* to show how to make yourself understood.

Done right, networking is fundamentally collaborational. Done wrong, networking adds to the abusive practices that have made many potentially valuable contacts defensive and suspicious. In one's work life, finding a fit is more important than merely landing a job, and the informal aspects of interpersonal relationships frequently decide whether there is a fit. If a job seeker shades the truth and creates an unrealistic picture of himself as a "product" simply to attract job offers, two things will happen when he gets an offer and accepts the job:

1. The employer will soon see that he didn't get what he bargained for, and that will make him mad.

2. The employer will realize that the job seeker deliberately fudged the truth, and that will make him madder. His trust in his new employee will be permanently destroyed. No trust, no fit, and, before long, no job.

Play the devil's advocate as you read this book. Turn up your skepticism and keep asking three fundamental questions:

1. Does this stuff make sense?
2. Will it work in the real world?
3. Can I learn to do it without stumbling or blushing?

Long before you turn the last page, you'll conclude that the editors of the *National Business Employment Weekly* were right: you can make networking the most effective tool in your job search arsenal.

"Oh, one more thing . . . one of the jurors wants to know if there's still an opening left from that accountant you murdered?"

1

What Networking Is . . . and What It's Not

Defining Our Terms

In the context of your job search or career transition, networking can best be described as the systematic development and cultivation of informal interpersonal contacts and relationships for three purposes:

1. To compile information that helps with focusing your job search objectives, learning about trends, events or facts relevant to your search, and, if you're really lucky, hearing about existing job openings;

2. To gain as much exposure as possible in the job market;

3. To gather more names and referrals so that you can continue to expand your network, gain more information sources, get more exposure, obtain still more referrals, and so on.

The crucial word in this definition is *systematic*. What many job seekers call networking is often no more than sporadic and disorganized badgering of a few relatives or friends with a desperate plea: "Do you know of anyone who has any openings for someone like me? . . . No? Well, if you hear of anything, would you let me know?"

This hit-or-miss approach, particularly if you don't communicate your job search objectives clearly or if you imply that you're willing to take any job that comes along, may produce an occasional lucky accident, but it's not an effective way to develop a variety of opportunities. No wonder so many disillusioned would-be networkers give up in disgust, take the first position that's offered and are heard to say, "I tried that whole networking thing with my friends and it didn't produce anything."

Skillful networking may appear low-key and informal, but it's not just a matter of randomly calling a few friends in the hope of a magical rescue from the miseries of the job market. It's a planned, structured and very time-consuming campaign that usually starts with friends, acquaintances and relatives (this stage is often called "contact development"), but rapidly moves on to meetings with people you don't know, who refer you to still more people you don't know. If you follow the maxim that a successful networking meeting is one that yields two more names than you went in with, you'll see a rapid geometric progression in your sources of information and your opportunities for market exposure. This multiplication effect produces greater knowledge, deeper perspective, more choices and, above all, the feeling that you're in control of the job search process and have left almost nothing to chance.

In a world where all the valuable information and attractive job openings aren't neatly organized like supermarket aisles, your best chance for success is to do anything and everything you can to get the word out and bring the information in. An effective job search is basically a numbers game: you have to play a lot of numbers to have the best chance of winning the game.

You will reach a point in your job search where all the broad-scale information you've gathered will help you to narrow your focus and to define your objectives succinctly. At that point, when your local library and other usual sources are no help, networking can be a remarkable vehicle for tracking down specific pieces of information. Want to know the name of the new Director of Field Service Engineering for Worldwide Oil Well Services? Need to wangle an introduction to the Managing Partner of a new venture capital firm? Friend-of-a-friend introductions are a major part of networking's operational repertoire.

Where Did Networking Come From?

Thirty years ago, the word *networking* wasn't in the common parlance of the job seeker. "Normal" people found jobs through ads. "Top executives" were placed by headhunters. College graduates and entry-level applicants flooded the job market with hundreds of form letters stapled to exuberant resumes. That was how it was done then. Life was simple.

Headhunters changed all that when the executive search industry went through a period of dramatic growth. As they conducted high-stakes searches, the headhunters soon learned that working informally through contacts was the best and fastest way to get valid information and identify attractive candidates. Placing ads produced a need to screen hundreds of resumes, each of which depicted a "bottom-line-oriented, shirtsleeved go-getter." The anecdotal information derived from informal chats and contacts often unearthed the best talent and gave a much more accurate picture of candidates' strengths and weaknesses. (Most major headhunters don't welcome unsolicited resumes, and many throw them away without reading them.)

Headhunters rapidly refined informal gossip into an art form, a creative technique. They found that they didn't have to begin with known contacts. Starting absolutely cold and using networking phone calls (one person suggests another person, who suggests another, and so on), a skilled researcher at an executive search firm often can identify several qualified candidates within a couple of hours. In these calls, the headhunters aren't dealing with the polished and sanitized information presented in resumes and cover letters; they're getting subjective, personalized opinions that often paint a far more accurate picture ("Stan is a marvelous planner and a good financial guy but he seems to have real difficulty working with self-confident women"). Another advantage of skilled networking is that it develops *good* information, not just a lot of information.

What Does Networking Look Like?

Picture yourself engaged in a brief, informal, face-to-face meeting and you'll be picturing yourself networking. As we'll see in later chapters, a lot of thought goes into planning, scheduling and orchestrating networking meetings, but the main mechanism is people chatting with people. Networking is essentially a social activity. It can be done by phone or letter, but it gets stiff and creaky when subjected to too much formality, lofty rhetoric or the confines of the written page. Because it's rooted in human nature, networking brings out the best and worst in people.

As in other expressions of human nature, we see a strange mix of altruism and self-interest, logic and irrationality, integrity and pettiness. Networking can be exhilarating and uplifting, or it can produce hurt, frustration and anger. Expect those results going in and you'll be all right.

The great networking adventure can include a fair amount of happenstance and coincidence: overhearing chance comments on a commuter train, running into a college roommate on a street corner, seeing an intriguing item in *The Wall Street Journal,* getting a bit of gossip by phone from a breathless friend. Networking is built on information and comes into play whenever and however information is shared. Remember: You may receive information from unplanned and unexpected places, but it's the systematic, planned use of that information that makes networking more effective than any other job search technique.

Over the years, networking has moved from use to overuse and then to frequent abuse. The word has become a cliché, a catchall for a variety of activities that don't even remotely resemble the planning and organization of a structured campaign to gather and disseminate information. Unless you consider *any* informal, interpersonal contact as part of networking, for example, you can hardly consider the practice of swapping business cards at a singles bar as effective networking. True, the primary vehicle for the networking process is an informal, brief, face-to-face meeting; but *an effective networking meeting has a predetermined purpose, a structure and an agenda.* Slipping your resume under someone's vodka gimlet doesn't qualify.

Another common misconception is that networking involves asking a lot of people whether they have any existing job openings. This isn't networking at all; it's another technique called *direct contact.* Whether you use mass mailings, targeted letters or face-to-face interaction, direct contact is a straight-out request for employment. By contrast, networking involves the sharing of information.

With direct contact, the underlying question is: "Can you employ me, here and now?" Everyone shies away from such high-stakes solicitation, especially people who know you and really would like to help you but can't. If you're unemployed, have you noticed how many of your friends seem to be avoiding you? They're afraid you're going to dash up to them, drop to your knees (figuratively), and beg them to rescue you. Odds are they can't do much to help at the moment. By asking for a level of help they can't provide, you provoke enormous guilt in them. They find it easier to stay away from you than risk experiencing such discomfort.

One major reason why networking is getting a bad name is that too many job seekers disguise direct contact overtures as networking meetings, thereby making a high-stakes confrontation out of what was supposed to be a low-key get-together. In one job search seminar, participants were being instructed on how to "decompress" a request for a networking meeting with a gentle disclaimer, such as, "Let me emphasize that, in asking for this meeting, I don't expect you to have a job for me or even to know of any openings. At this point in my job search, my purpose is to get some advice, a little market exposure, and perhaps the names of a few people I could call to expand my network of contacts."

A contemptuous snort came from the back of the room. "I could never say that!" boomed one participant. "I am looking for a job! I'm not going to lie like that."

He was absolutely right. If you think there might be an opening or opportunity with a certain employer, it is devious to use a networking request as a subterfuge to get a quick-and-dirty job interview. Suppose, however, in a networking meeting, someone suddenly says, "Gee, we really could use someone with your credentials. What would you think about working in a place like this?" Great! At that point, you're not networking anymore; you've entered interview country. But unless and until the other person raises the ante, it's up to you to keep the networking meeting low-pressure, informal and conversational. There's nothing illicit about direct contact and no sin in directly requesting employment if you think someone might have an opening. But direct contact and networking are fundamentally different techniques, and job seekers confuse them at their peril.

In this same vein, *networking isn't interviewing*. An interview is a high-stakes negotiating session in which someone is trying to decide whether you're worth a lot of a company's money. A networking meeting is a low-stakes conversation that works best if almost nothing is involved except a few minutes of the contact's time. An interview is the potential employer's meeting: he or his representative sets the agenda, drives it and is responsible for its outcome. A networking meeting is your meeting. It is a favor someone has granted to you, and it's your responsibility to make sure it goes only where it should.

For this reason, you should eliminate the phrase "informational interview" from your vocabulary. A few years ago, this was another name for a networking meeting, but the term encourages confused agendas. If the phrase is supposed to suggest an interview where nothing is at stake, it's an oxymoron.

The Miner versus the Antenna

It's amazing that networking gets such good results when almost every new job seeker misunderstands how networking works. Networking can be built on two fundamental mechanisms: (1) mining the market and (2) tuning in antennas. Too many people appreciate only the mining mechanism—the less effective of the two.

Most candidates see the job market as a huge, overhanging mountain. They stand at the foothills, unable to see over, around or into the mountain. But they know that somewhere in that mountain are nuggets of gold—first-rate opportunities or sensational job openings. But where? No map of the mountain is available, and there's no way to fly over it or x-ray it to find its treasures.

The job seeker—let's call him JS—grabs a trusty pick and shovel and begins to dig a mineshaft into the mountain. When he's under way, say at point A, his brother-in-law Al, who's a nice guy and eager to help, sends in a message. Al knows of no positive pathways to the treasures, but he suggests that JS try to intersect the pact of his friend, Becky. JS thanks Al and directs his mineshaft over to Becky. She proves friendly (she used to date Al) and says she'll call ahead to introduce JS to her boss, Chuck, who has several connecting mineshafts. JS thanks her, bids her adieu, and hacks out a tunnel that brings him to Chuck. Chuck refers JS to Deirdre, who starts a chain of referrals: Deirdre to Ellen; Ellen to Fred; Fred to Greg; Greg to Herman; and so on.

JS is doing his part. He's digging and shoveling like crazy, tracking down the leads each referral provides, and initiating contact with lots of people. Eventually, Marvin refers him to Nancy, who looks at his resume and exclaims: "What a happy concidence! We're looking for someone exactly like you!" JS throws away his pick and shovel and prepares to get on with his work life.

In this mining metaphor, *JS is doing all the work*. He's the only one gathering information, and the scope of his networking is limited only by how much time he has to dig tunnels and mineshafts, and how many people he can reach in that amount of time.

This model assumes that, in the meetings with JS, each person contacted has provided all the help he or she is ever going to be able to give. After they refer JS to someone else, his networking contacts might as well be dead for all he cares. JS keeps shoveling frantically forward toward the next contact. He never looks back, revisits an earlier dig, or checks to be sure he hasn't dug a huge circle.

Done this way—and only this way—networking uses up a lot of time and energy, yet it still produces its share of hits. Dig long and hard enough with the

---

FOR YOUR INFORMATION

THE MEMORY TRACE

People often "file" things mentally using visual cues, so it's important to meet people face to face when you're networking. But remember, the first impression is a lasting one. Setting your hair on fire in a networking meeting will definitely get you remembered, but it probably won't lead to many referrals.

Figure 1.1 The Four Network Categories

Your Network of Personal Relationships
☆ Immediate family
☆ Relatives, near and far
☆ Close friends, neighbors and casual acquaintances
☆ Distant friends, old friends, ex-roommates, old flames, drinking buddies, fair weather friends
☆ Your personal doctor, lawyer, dentist, accountant, insurance agent, broker, personal banker, beautician, barber, manicurist, tailor, acupuncturist, rolfer, masseur, mechanic
☆ Your minister, priest, rabbi, psychologist, psychiatrist or counselor
☆ Members of country clubs, social clubs, fraternal organizations, recreational groups, school parent groups, sports teams or mountain-climbing expeditions

Your Network of Professional Relationships
☆ Colleagues in your organization: Superiors, subordinates, peers, secretaries, support staff
☆ Colleagues in other organizations: Customers, clients, collaborators
☆ Vendors, consultants, contractors, lawyers, accountants, investment bankers, lessors, lessees
☆ Competitors and professional acquaintances
☆ Joint venturers, investors, shareholders
☆ Lobbyists, regulators and licensors
☆ Your advertising agency, PR firm or marketing representative

Your Network of Organizational and Community Affiliations
☆ Boards of directors, boards of trustees and advisory boards
☆ Community or volunteer organizations
☆ Professional, cultural and civic organizations
☆ Philanthropic organizations
☆ Fundraising groups
☆ Public-private consortiums; business development organizations; chambers of commerce
☆ Certifying or licensing bodies

Opportunistic Networks
☆ That guy you met on the 5:15 to White Plains
☆ The pedestrian you just hit with your car who turns out to be your brother-in-law's college roommate
☆ The fellow who runs the newsstand
☆ The couple with the season tickets next to you who hate the Lakers almost as much as you do
☆ The other woman bumped off Flight 962
☆ All 213 other participants in the "Self-Realization for the 90s" seminar
☆ All your granfalloons (See Chapter 10)

mining-the-market mechanism and you'll eventually reach some gold. This is the restricted image most job seekers have of networking: a sweaty, tiring activity that has a sizable risk of missing gold altogether.

Now compare the mining mechanism to the antenna mechanism (and assume that JS mends some of his ways). After JS meets with Al, Al doesn't just vanish or die. He goes on living, attending lunches, crossing paths with colleagues, overhearing and spreading gossip. If JS has made a positive impression on Al by painting a succinct and attractive picture of his skills and abilities, his image is now etched indelibly in Al's mind, whether Al likes it or not.

In 1990s terminology, JS has "programmed" Al and Al has become an antenna tuned to receive signals on JS's "channel." When Al hears a bit of information that "twangs" that channel, he will attend to it in a way he never did before his meeting with JS. In the course of all his networking, JS has created a whole bunch of antennas, all tuned to his wavelength. Instead of relying solely on his own ears, he now has the potential benefit of scores, even hundreds of listeners.

To correct his earlier mistake, JS has to go back to retrieve the information. If Al hears of a job opening that's a perfect fit for JS, he may take the time to give him a call (he knows that if he's responsible for his brother-in-law's landing well, JS will be beholden to him forever). Less earth-shaking information may get remarked on and filed for a while by JS's other contacts, but if they don't hear from JS, then JS never gets the information. Opportunities may have been missed before by not checking in periodically with Becky and Chuck and all the other "antennae." JS knows better now. He keeps his channel active and stays in touch with all his contacts.

What Is a Network, Anyway?

We started this chapter with a formal definition of *networking,* but it's important to nail down just what a *network* is. Think of a network as any group of people you know or can get to know for the purposes of sharing information. Every network is based on some form of interpersonal relationship, and each of us has a variety of networks operating at different levels and in different locations. Think of some of your possibilities: the people you vacation with, the network of vendors who provided your last employer with goods and services, your colleagues in your trade association, your family, your past and present clients, your fellow board members at a corporation or nonprofit foundation, and numerous other contacts—some formal, some informal; some long-lasting, some fleeting; some current, some dormant; some deeply meaningful, some excruciatingly superficial.

To make the concept of a network manageable, it's best to separate your present and potential network members into four general categories: (1) **Personal**, (2) **Professional**, (3) **Organizational** and (4) **"Opportunistic."**

Look at the lists of people you know in these four categories, and you'll realize that you regularly associate with a lot of potential networking contacts—and could reach many more by expending a little more effort. There will be some overlap among the four categories: you socialize with your colleagues at the laboratory, you choose a close friend as your investment banker, and you see a lot of business colleagues at the monthly Chamber of Commerce lunch.

Each of your four main networks will have some distinctive features, however. Your **Personal Network** will include people who never see you with your "game face" on; that is, they don't encounter you in your employment capacity, and the relationship they enjoy with you is anchored in interpersonal bonds or personal service relationships. This is important because if you're using networking for career development and employment purposes, your game face is what you're selling.

Your friends and relatives may care about you, want to help you, and feel a real stakeholding in your well-being. But they're not accustomed to thinking of you as a "product," and if asked to tell someone what you do for a living, they may have a hard time giving a succinct and accurate description. In later chapters, we'll look at the technique for networking among your various constituencies. For now, remember: Your friends know you only in the way they know you.

The members of your **Professional Network** may also have an incomplete view of everything you are and do, but at least what they see is your "game face." They see you at work, and they can convey their opinion of the way you work. Often, they can understand the technical details of your profession when even your spouse can't describe your job duties exactly. Professional relationships tend to be more structured than personal ones, which generally puts a more "businesslike" face on networking among professional acquaintances. In describing you to others or others to you, they'll tend to focus on what you do more than on who you are.

Most organizations have various "subnetworks" whose function is the dissemination of informal information and protocols and/or the preservation of power. They have familiar labels: The Old Boys Network, The Keepers of the Glass Ceiling, The Grapevine, The Minority and The Women's Straight Talk Network, All Those Who Hate Management, and others. They don't figure in the networking techniques described in this book because, in most cases, the very existence of such "subnetworks" is denied. Members of these groups share valuable information with whom they want, not with outsiders asking for favors. Their goal is exclusivity, not accessibility.

Your **Organizational Network** will overlap heavily with your Professional Network. In your organizational affiliations—business associations, community groups, foundations, professional groups, boards of directors, boards of trustees—you may again be showing a face that is different from the one you display at the office or the one you show to your personal contacts. Here again, the opinions expressed about you or about networking contacts within these groups will reflect strengths and deficits in the organizational setting. A mediocre lawyer may be a superb motivator for United Way; a high-profile female executive may earn a lot of respect on Wall Street but be criticized for her half-hearted participation in the several nonprofit boards on which she serves.

"Other" relationships—those that defy categorization—can add real spice to life. These are the chance connections, the unexpected coincidences, the ships passing in the night, the accidental conversation partners who are never seen again. They can include superficial relationships with a large group (all your fourth-grade classmates, for example) or deep, highly individual bonds (the woman whose baby you helped deliver in the taxicab last year).

Taken together, your networks form a rich tapestry. Until you list all the personal relationships you can tap into for your job search, you cannot know their breadth and depth. Most job seekers tend to underestimate the enormous potential of their networks, particularly their personal or family networks. "My cousin Myron? Hah! That idiot doesn't know anything! There's no point in wasting my time on him. I need to get in front of the people with clout, the people who can make things happen."

You're right in wanting to network with the movers and shakers, particularly after you've used earlier networking efforts to clarify your focus and hone your self-presentation. But don't forget that Myron has eyes and ears; he may not be a great antenna, but he's still an extension of your information-gathering resources. Include him! He sees a lot of people you don't see and he goes to a lot of places you don't go.

Every member of your personal, professional, organizational, and opportunistic networks is a possible antenna. Accept one of the great frustrations of the networking game: you don't know when it's going to work. Hundreds of contacts, meetings, and conversations may appear to have produced little. Then Myron may call unexpectedly to tell you about an interesting conversation he overheard in the order line at Burger King. Skillful networkers know they *can't push* the process, they can only *do* the process. They work their prime contacts as adroitly as they can, but they keep in mind a key principle in maximizing job market exposure: There can be enormous strength in weak ties.

Carefully cultivated networks offer one other benefit that often is overlooked by job seekers in the heat of the campaign: after you find a new job, you still have your networks. Candid information is essential in all walks of life, and an essential discipline of successful people is the care and feeding of their networks. When they've found a satisfying new position, many former job seekers let their networks rust among the weeds. Maintaining networks is as much a systematic and structured process as creating them.

One Philadelphia lawyer, a marvelous networker who managed the nearly impossible task of moving into law firm practice after starting her career in-house and spending eight years there, is adamant that every name in her revolving file gets at least two phone calls, one letter, and a holiday card each year. This is a lot of work, and she's not even looking for a job! She's doing business development for her firm, and she is doing just fine: She's a highly visible figure in her business community. People seek her out for information and, in the course of doing so, they provide her with a lot of information. She's dialed-in, hooked-up, on top, in control.

"If you're going to spend all that time and effort meeting a lot of people during your job search," she says, "it makes no sense to throw all that effort away after you land."

2

Defining and Redefining the Product

Tell me about yourself.

There it is: the simple request that induces anxiety in even the most focused job seekers, and generates almost total mental paralysis in career changers. One of the basic purposes of networking is to trigger as much exposure in the job market as possible, so you're left with the question of what to expose. No matter how benignly expressed, the demand to explain yourself resonates with a number of implicit subdemands:

☆   "Be focused. Be self-aware. Don't ask *me* to make sense of your life."

☆   "Be succinct; don't give me a lot of abstract babble."

☆   "Don't jive with me. Your tale had better be objective and credible."

☆   "What do you offer? What value can you add?"

☆   "Explain why you want what you want."

The tell-me-about-yourself request is the real beginning of most interviews, and it's also one of the first hurdles that should be approached in any networking meeting. Knowing the request is coming and knowing how to fulfill it are two different things. Avoid the most frequently given response: "Well, what do you want to know?" This counterquestion, which throws the responsibility back to the questioner, might be paraphrased, "That question is so stupid I can't even begin to answer it." In networking, it's a particularly abrasive response because you, the networker, asked for the meeting and should have an agenda in mind. One memorable real-life networking exchange went like this:

Networker (NW)*:* Thank you for taking the time to see me on such short notice. [This isn't a bad start.]

Contact (C)*:* You're welcome. How can I help you? [Also a good opener.]

NW (rattled)*:* Well, I was hoping you could help me in my job search.

C (patiently)*:* I'll do what I can. Why don't you tell me a little about yourself?

NW: What do you want to know?

C: What do you want me to know?

NW: I don't understand.

C: Neither do I.

NW (panicking)*:* No . . . I mean . . . I thought you were going to help me.

C: I'm trying, but I don't know enough about you to know where to start. You're running a job search, right? You're marketing a "product"?

NW: Yeah . . . .

C (voice rising)*:* So what's the product?!

NW (defensive)*:* If I knew that, I wouldn't be networking with you.

C: Look: you can't just come in here, dump your bucket on my desk, and expect me to put it all together for you.

Believe me, it didn't get any better after this initial exchange. The networker thought the contact was hostile and unhelpful; the contact considered the networker to be unprepared, unfocused and unwilling to carry his responsibility for keeping the meeting on track. As a networker, you really must be able to do better.

Start by Determining What You Want

You're probably anxious at this point to start creating a whole series of new antennas for yourself. But you can't tune a lot of people to your networking wavelength if your transmission is fuzzy or if no one knows what channel you're on.

Perhaps you have already worked through a detailed self-assessment and vocational profiling and are brimming with articulate self-awareness. Or, perhaps you're among those rare people who are so gifted with innate insight that they know every nook and cranny of their personal profiles. If you fit into either of these categories, the topics in this chapter may be familiar, but you'll learn some of the vocabulary we'll be using, the issues that will get primary focus, and some methods for making job seekers incredibly self-aware.

Establishing a Frame of Reference

Anyone who has lived long enough to reach job hunting age has gained, from experience, some sense of his strengths, aptitudes, hot buttons, soft spots and danger zones. In other words, most adults *are* self-aware, at least at some semiconscious, nonverbal level. That doesn't mean they can articulate their self-understanding succinctly on demand, however. Before you start scheduling networking meetings, you have to spend time learning to (1) think of yourself as an attractive product and (2) describe yourself clearly as that product.

This is easier said than done. Each of us is a complex amalgam of forces and factors, a unique blend of nature, nurture, education, experience and operative values. Confronted with the need to present an articulate and attractive personal profile (actually, a "product profile"; we mustn't forget that we're selling a product to a market), many of us act like a deer caught in headlights. What do I put first? What comes last? How much detail do I put in? What do I leave out? How do I organize what stays in—chronologically or the most important stuff first? Should I build to a big finish?

The best way to understand how people—networking contacts and potential employers alike—will size you up is to reflect on how you size up other people. When you first meet someone in a business context, what information do you want to know first? What data are essential to describing someone clearly as a product? Consider the following descriptions:

> I met this extraordinary woman at the conference, Bill. She got out of Wesleyan about the same time as your brother Len, got her Master's in Planning from

---

FOR YOUR INFORMATION

CAREER PROFILE (ON A RESUME)

Sixteen years of diverse financial management and investment banking experience, most recently as partner and chief financial officer of the nation's fifth largest commercial real estate developer. Previous experience as controller of a publicly held regional engineering firm and as a mergers/acquisitions consultant with a Big Six consulting firm.

Ohio State, spent a couple of years at HUD, then left to start her own city planning consulting firm. In two years, she already has major contracts with Dubuque and Spokane. After initially doing everything herself, she now does all the research and writing and has a staff of four—all women with major smarts, like her—who run the office and do the project administration.

———

"Nice party."

"Yeah. Great hors d'oeuvres."

"So. What do you do?"

"I'm an outplacement consultant with one of the big New York career consulting firms."

"No kidding. Maybe I should ask you to find me a job. How long you been at it?"

"Only about three years, actually."

"And before that?"

"Well, I started my career as a minister, up in Maine. While I was chaplain at a prison up there, I put in a lot of educational programs, and they asked me to become assistant warden. Did that for about eight years—actually left the ministry, although I still did a lot of counseling. By then I had a family and needed more income, and a guy who knew my work asked me if I wanted to join the human resources department at a Fortune 150 company's marine colloid division in Portland. It was a big change, but I really enjoyed the job until I was transferred to Philadelphia. That got old real fast, but I was doing a lot of career and family counseling on the side, and I liked that. Met a guy at a conference who asked me if I wanted to combine everything I've ever done into one job, and boom! I was an outplacement consultant. Go figure."

If you look closely at these profiles, you'll notice that each provides a **Frame Of Reference** (F.O.R.). (Remember this phrase; we're going to beat it to death in this book.) The F.O.R. is anchored in three dimensions, each of which addresses fundamental questions that must be answered in order to describe someone (including yourself) as a product:

1. Level

How much experience do you have?

How flat or how steep is your learning curve?

How much money is it going to cost to employ you?

2. Roles and functions

Exactly what can you do for your next employer?

What is your primary area of competency?

What other skills and abilities can you contribute?

How do you most want to be used?

3. Setting

Where have you performed most recently, and how similar was that setting to the one in which you're now seeking employment?

What earlier settings did you perform in?

What does the chronology of settings in which you've worked during your career imply about the kind of setting you most *like* working in?

Unless and until a listener has at least some information on all of these areas—level, roles and functions and setting—he's missing crucial pieces of your profile and can't describe you to someone else—or decide that he might want to employ you himself.

Conveying your F.O.R. doesn't have to be a lengthy process. Say you meet an old friend in a movie line, and she says, "What do you do?" You don't have a half hour to flesh out the details, but in one or two sentences you can provide enough general information to create a basic product profile:

> For the past eight years, I've been in charge of sales support for a small importer of Tibetan toupees in Topeka. Mainly, I organize and track the new leads generated by customer information cards in *GQ, Tonsorial Monthly* and *Modern Maturity* magazines.

Level (eight years), roles and functions (manage the sales support) and setting (small Topeka importer) are all there. Based on this brief but pithy movie-line summary, perhaps you'll get a call from her brother, the product manager for a whole line of personal grooming products at Gillette. This sort of thing happens all the time—but not if you can't teach others how to describe you in the three essential dimensions.

Level can be suggested in many ways: number of years out of college or grad school, job title, scope of authority, age, budget responsibility you've had, and so on. For career changers, however, the question of level poses an interesting problem: an individual can be very experienced in a prior role or setting, and can have tons of life-tempered judgment and street smarts, and still be an absolute beginner in a newly chosen field. An employer will therefore have to expend some time and money developing these new competencies, but he'll be investing those resources on a mature, motivated person (you have to be motivated to make a major career change). How much "credit" should be given for a high level of authority or responsibility in a prior work life? Any career changer's F.O.R. has to anticipate and address that question.

Roles and functions are straightforward: What is it you can do? What value do you bring to the employer? Can you prove it? Like the movie-line example above, this description can be short and tight. Generally speaking, however, the more time you have to explain your F.O.R. (two minutes? ten minutes? a whole hour?), the more *action verbs* you should add. Why action verbs? What you are describing is activity. Too many people tend to describe themselves in terms of "I am"; it's far more effective to describe yourself in terms of "I do."

> "I manage the compensation and benefits function."
> "I evaluate potential merger and acquisition targets."
> "I operate a fish processing company."
> "I drive the little circus clown car with the other 25 clowns tucked in behind me."

Action verbs get remembered. Passive verbs don't.

The issue of motivation enters into roles and functions. There's an enormous difference between what someone is capable of doing and what they're temperamentally suited to do (which is why more than two-thirds of the people surveyed in the United States routinely say they dislike their jobs). Someone's functional resume, for example, may list five or six areas of competency—administration, staff development, treasury, management information systems (MIS), human resources (HR), project management—but no relative pecking order is given for these claimed functional competencies. Which does the person do best? Which does he want to do most?

The question of *setting* focuses not on what you can do but on where you want to do it. A potential employer wants to know all about your last work setting in order to compare it with the possible new setting. The more similar the two settings are in their nature, scope and operative features, the more the employer can infer that whatever you accomplished there you can accomplish again. Because employers are natural risk-reducers, this is a logical inquiry.

A review of your prior work settings also can reveal a lot about your motivational map. Where you chose to work—and how long you stayed in each setting—can send some pretty strong signals that certain kinds of settings are comfortable and highly motivating for you, and others are turnoffs. If your resume shows that you worked two years in the private sector, then the next 16 years in the world of nonprofit foundations, isn't the reader entitled to infer something about your value system? Or, if your career path starts with a Fortune 500 multinational, heads off into a specialized division, does a one-eighty into a start-up consulting firm with 15 employees and no job titles, and finally levels off into a sole proprietorship, isn't it fair to assume that your career path expresses a "theory of choices" and is relevant to the kind of setting you'd be happy in?

The problem this issue poses for career changers is obvious. A conventional job seeker who presents a linear career profile—ever-increasing responsibilities in a progression of roles in generally similar settings—is easy to pigeonhole. The F.O.R. is clear and unambiguous. But when confronted with someone who's making a major shift in level, role or setting, the job market raises some immediate alarms: Is this a flight *to* something or *from* something? Why move away from the stability and comfort of an established career identity? Is this a rational, reasoned move or an impulsive symptom of a midcareer crisis?

Career changers, in effect, have to be ready with two F.O.R.s: one that describes their past work life and another that describes their future objectives. They also have to be ready with a "bridge"—a credible explanation of the factors and timing that have led to their decision to make a change.

The Product Profile: Pieces of the puzzle

By now it has probably dawned on you that your frame of reference isn't a complete product description of all you are and all you have to offer; it's the tightest, most abbreviated version of you that is still able to sketch a market identity. It's an essential first step, not the last word. When someone on the commuter train tells you, "I've been Director of New Product Development of a billion-dollar multinational chemical manufacturer for 10 years," she's inviting you to pigeonhole her in terms of generic categories. Her F.O.R. tells you she's in a line management job, not a staff job; that she's in chemicals, not pharmaceuticals or consumer products; that she has functioned long and successfully in a large, bureaucratic organization; and that she's an experienced manager and not a freshly minted MBA.

Suppose, however, that she was in the running for a new position where every one of her competitors was basically like her: an experienced new product development director in a major corporation. Now the question becomes: What traits, features and accomplishments distinguish her from other, similar people? In this context, the request to "Tell me about yourself" demands a much greater level of detail. Without some intensive, structured self-assessment before the job search begins (and before networking commences in earnest), you cannot hope to present a clear, confident, and controlled rendition of "Me, the Product."

Ask Not What Others Can Do for You . . .

This is a good time to clarify who's responsible for what in the networking process. Through networking, you can acquire information that will help focus, clarify and reality-test your career or job search objectives, but you must understand that it isn't the duty of networking contacts to substitute their judgment for your own self-analysis. The initial responsibility for figuring yourself out is yours, and you should come to your networking contacts prepared to say, in effect, "I've done my homework, and everything points to my being competent and happy doing _____. I'd welcome your thoughts on whether this is realistic and, if so, how I might best translate my objectives into appropriate employment." This is not the same as saying, "Gee, Charlie, I'm utterly lost. What should I do with my life?"

There are a number of approaches to conducting a detailed, objective vocational assessment. You can stand in front of your bathroom mirror and shout, "Mirror, mirror, tell me true, what in God's name shall I do?" You can buy any of a number of self-assessment books or one of the increasingly popular software programs that will work you through a series of questions or exercises intended to get you to look systematically at your strengths, preferences and weaknesses.

Such solo approaches are subject to two major problems: (1) "garbage in, garbage out" and (2) overidealization (sometimes called "kidding yourself" or "reinventing yourself"). Both of these forms of distortion can be diminished by enlisting some form of outside help—a cool-headed spouse or significant other, a trusted friend, a support group, or a professional career counselor—to serve as an objective sounding board.

The self-assessment process can be entirely subjective and qualitative, or it can include administration and feedback of a variety of standardized instruments that measure everything from intelligence and personality preferences to interest patterns and operative value systems.

Although a detailed discussion of career reappraisal and vocational/skills assessment is beyond the scope of this book, we can talk generally about self-profiling. How can your assessment information be organized and presented for the best possible communication to networking contacts and potential employers? In response to "Tell me about yourself—in detail," too many people lump distinctly different kinds of attributes together in a kind of undifferentiated hash. You'll be far clearer—and feel far more in control—if you learn to keep your ingredients separate.

TSs, TAs and PQs

Every person's work identity can be described as a combination of three ingredients:

1. Technical skills (TSs);
2. Transferable abilities (TAs);
3. Personal qualities (PQs).

Different kinds of jobs can involve distinctly different percentages of each of these ingredients—a nuclear energy plant's control room operator uses heavy TSs, a poet's work requires a reservoir of PQs—but some mixture of these basic vocational building blocks is present in any viable job candidate.

When we speak of technical skills here, we're using the word *skill* in a particular way, not simply as another word for *competency*. For our purposes, a technical skill is a body of knowledge, and the way you describe a technical skill is to say "I know it." For example: "I know Lotus 1-2-3" or "I know Russian" or "I know the federal regulations that govern the interstate transportation of chickens" or "I know what every switch and light in this nuclear control room does." Another word for technical skill is "expertise." Here are some other examples of TSs:

☆ Fourth-generation computer languages.
☆ Organic chemistry.
☆ The rules of contract bridge.
☆ The maximum rpm of the Model 3600 drill press.
☆ Third-party reimbursement procedures under Medicare.

☆   The military specifications governing procurement of hammers.

☆   Federal law governing Superfund cleanup of toxic waste dump sites.

☆   Generally accepted accounting principles (GAAP).

☆   The molecular structure of DNA.

☆   The current trade protocols within the European Community.

Get the idea? When asked to describe themselves, many people naturally start by describing areas of technical expertise. Why? Because expertise tends to be yes-or-no: either you know something or you don't. If I were to put a gun to some poor networker's head and say, "You have 15 seconds to list your primary areas of expertise," chances are the person would survive. Most people can describe their TSs pretty well, even under stress.

A word often substituted for technical skills is *credentials*—specific references to a job seeker's formal educational background. Education frequently has little predictive validity for on-the-job success, yet many shortsighted employers fixate on credentials: "Where'd you go to school? What was your grade-point average? What were your scores on the SATs?" They *think* they're asking, "What do you know?" A petty overreliance on credentials is one of the major blind spots of the job market and the hiring process.

Some interesting characteristics of technical skills may not be readily evident, but are important to constructing a vocational profile. First, a young person can know a given technical skill just as well as an older person (indeed, he often knows it better, perhaps because he just finished courses on the latest thinking in the field). Second, you can acquire more technical skills at any point in your career. If you want or need some kind of expertise or some new credentials badly enough, you can always go back to school, attend a seminar, or ask for on-the-job training. Want to start scuba diving? Go learn the skills in a scuba-diving class.

The third point requires a little thinking over: a technical skill creates a pigeonhole; it tends to define or be defined by the setting in which it's used. Here's what I mean. If I were to tell you, "I know COBOL," I would be placing myself, in your mind, in a room with an old-fashioned mainframe computer—the only setting in which that technical skill is relevant. COBOL has no value whatever on camping trips or in negotiations for collective bargaining agreements. If I say, "My practice requires expertise on the Federal Rules of Criminal Procedure," then (1) I am a lawyer, (2) I am a criminal lawyer and (3) I am a criminal lawyer practicing in federal court. That body of expertise probably does me little good in state court and none at all on the racquetball court.

Another way of making this point is to say that technical skills aren't transferable. One of their greatest virtues is that they define neat labels or categories that we can assign ourselves. When a doctor says, "I am a thoracic surgeon," he's telling you that he possesses at least the minimal amount of technical skills required to use that label to describe himself. He also is telling you what he isn't: he isn't a brain surgeon, he isn't an orthopedic surgeon, he isn't a radiologist.

For our model, technical skills are a logical first line of self-definition. How can you catalog your technical skills? Simple; get a piece of paper and a pen or pencil, sit down where you can write comfortably, and list them on the paper. (If it adds incentive, imagine a gun at your head.) If you're pursuing a linear career path, focus on those TSs that are relevant to your calling or area of expertise. If you're thinking of making a career shift (or are feeling low in the self-esteem department), broaden your inventory to include all the areas in which you have technical skills. Do you know how to cross-pollinate an orchid? Know how to mix a high-fire ceramic glaze? Know what kind of crown moulding was used in English architecture between 1790 and 1830? Know the best mixture of cheeses for making a great lasagna? Once you start listing your technical skills, you'll be amazed at all the things you know.

Next, you have to do some prioritizing. You aren't going to sell *all* your technical skills to your next employer, so choose the ones that best define your fundamental product identity. Which will be most important, or absolutely required, when you are considered for a position in your line of work? When you've completed and prioritized your list, create a vocational profile template like the one shown in Table 2.1, and write your technical skills into the left-hand column.

Once they've tallied their technical skills—"described my credentials," they may call it—many people think their self-assessment is done. They've defined the product; now it's time to start networkin' and job searchin'. Wrong.

Your technical skills tell the job market only whether you're entitled to play. If you lack the technical skills a certain job requires, by definition you're incompetent for that job. The rest of your profile, no matter how attractive, is irrelevant. The vertical line in Table 2.1 is meant to represent a "screen," as in the screening interview, screening out the turkeys, a screening ad, and so on.

A demon set of credentials (your 4.0 from MIT as a nuclear physics major) will get you through the screen faster than a mediocre set (your 2.4 in underwater basket weaving from Larry, Moe and Curley's Threeway University), but it doesn't determine your overall attractiveness to the job market, and it certainly doesn't define the kind of setting in which you'd be happiest or most productive.

One common job search myth is that "the best qualified person gets the job." If that translates to "the person with the snazziest technical skills will always prevail," it's not true. At some point, you've probably received some version of this letter:

Table 2.1   Vocational Profile Template

Category	"CREDENTIALS"	"FIT"	
	TECHNICAL SKILLS (TSs)	TRANSFERABLE ABILITIES (TAs)	PERSONAL QUALITIES (PQs)
Common Term	Expertise	Experience, Judgment, Aptitude, Maturity	Preferences Temperament
Strength Reflected	"I know ＿＿＿＿" "I am a ＿＿＿＿	"I have done ＿＿＿" "I'm a natural at ＿＿＿＿"	"I am ＿＿＿" "I like ＿＿＿"
Examples	programming	trouble-shooting	creative
	Russian	tactical planning	initiating
	accounting	organizing	goal-oriented
	plumbing	collaborating	affiliating
	rocket science	interpersonal	conceptual
	brain surgery	abilities	entrepreneurial
	mass spectroscopy	assessing needs	self-starting
	corporate finance	setting goals	logical
	accounting	setting standards	analytical
	programming	setting priorities	practical
	computers	action planning	creative
	compensation/	implementing	loyal/committed
	benefits	organizing	good at theory
	commercial	scheduling	curious
	litigation	coordinating	fond of variety
	pharmaceutical	collaborating	comfortable
	research	leading	with change
	civil engineering	working well	reliable
	arbitrage	independently	willing to accept challenge
	environmental law	monitoring	or risk
	healthcare	troubleshooting	quick study
	reimbursement	problem solving	persevering
	marine biology	public speaking	patient
	administering	writing	persuasive
	trusts	interpersonal relations	project-oriented
	designing machines	managing time	process-oriented
	brain surgery	building trust	results-oriented
	appellate procedure	translating concepts	detail-oriented
	painting portraits	into action	concept-oriented
	administrative law	mastering new skills	reflective
		managing projects	outgoing/
		taking responsibility	affiliating
		marketing	energetic
		researching	ambitious

Dear Mr. Jones:

Although your credentials are indeed impressive, we have selected a candidate who better fits our needs. Best of luck in your future endeavors.

Frustrating, isn't it? What in the world do they mean by "fit" (or "chemistry" or "rapport" or other such vagaries)? The notion of "fit" strikes most of us as hopelessly subjective and another recipe for hash, rather like Supreme Court Justice Potter Stewart's definition of pornography: "I can't define it, but I know it when I see it." Are the ingredients of fit unknowable and uncontrollable? If we hit it off with a networking contact or a potential employer, is it strictly a matter of chance?

Figuring Out Fit

If the best qualified person *doesn't* always get the job, who does? The person who makes the employer most comfortable. What qualities make an employer most comfortable?

1. Strong evidence that the candidate can do what he claims; that he can add immediate, tangible value in exchange for the employer's bucks.
2. A personal style or a set of traits and values that are compatible with the employer's.

On the template in Table 2.1, the column to the left of the vertical line or "screen" is labeled "credentials," and the two columns to the right are labeled "fit." Once you're through the screen, you must get to the real heart of self-assessment and self-definition: What distinguishes you from all the other job seekers who may have similar credentials?

The first component on the "fit" side of the template is your particular array of transferable abilities (TAs). Let me emphasize that, in our nomenclature, skills and abilities are very different. If *expertise* is the synonym for a particular technical skill, then the synonym for transferable abilities is *experience*.

Suppose you say to me, "I have the ability to run a four-minute mile." All that phrase really means is, "I have run a four-minute mile at least once." Somewhere in your past (that is, in your experience) is a four-minute mile, and logic says that if you were able to do it once, presumably you can do it again. If I am an employer who runs a courier service and values employees who are fleet-of-foot, the best proof of what you can do for me is what you've done before. Remember this principle:

$$\text{Abilities} = \text{Past behaviors} = \text{Experience}$$

The best way to describe a transferable ability is to say, "I have done X," not "I know X." When someone says, in a networking meeting or in an interview, "I have the ability to keep my head when those about me lose theirs," he's paraphrasing some prior experience: "I have performed calmly in situations that involved great emotional stress."

If this line of logic holds true, then every job seeker naturally should be articulate at describing his abilities—his experience—right? Isn't he just describing accomplishments that have already happened? If you think it's all that easy for the average person to rattle off his abilities, imagine another gun at your temple and respond to this command:

In the next 30 seconds, please list your six most significant transferable abilities—*in priority order*. Ready? Go!

1. _____

2. _____

3. _____

4. _____

5. _____

6. _____

If your mind turned to cotton during this 30-second exercise, you're not alone. Most of us *are* self-aware; that is, we can remember the things we've done in our lives and we have clear images of the ones that turned out well. But having an implicit understanding of our past accomplishments doesn't mean that we can call those accomplishments up in our mind's eye on demand—and communicate them explicitly to someone else.

In this phase of your self-assessment process, your task is to inventory the experiences and accomplishments you've already had and learn to describe them in terms that are meaningful and attractive to the job market. Before we discuss how to do that, however, you may want to know where "transferable" comes into our discussion of transferable abilities.

Unlike technical skills, which tend to be anchored to a particular setting, transferable abilities aren't confined to any one job or situation. As an example, consider "troubleshooting," a classic transferable ability. If you turn into a demon troubleshooter when the document package for a real estate closing is missing a few pages, you'll find that same ability emerging when things threaten to get out of hand at a PTA meeting, or when the caterer delivers your daughter's wedding cake to the wrong house, or when the car starts making strange noises a half hour after you've passed the Last Chance Gas Station in the Nevada desert.

This element of transferability is the salvation of career changers. It is, first and foremost, what they have to learn to sell. Suppose you did a splendid job of planning and implementing a new employee assistance program at MegaBig Manufacturing. Isn't it fair to infer that you'd be pretty good at developing and running a community outreach program for your city's Department of Aging? Or developing a new tuition reimbursement program at your local university? Or helping to get an Outward Bound program up and running for inner-city kids?

The setting has changed (from private sector to government or academe or nonprofit human services), but the underlying ability—let's label it "program development"—is readily transferable. The trick, then, is to learn to describe your transferable abilities in terms that are succinct enough to register clearly in the mind of a networking contact or potential employer. The best way to do this is to think of your accomplishments and experiences in terms of their functional components. For example:

☆   The ability to organize complex data and information.
☆   The ability to organize the activities of people.
☆   The ability to build trust with people who don't know you.
☆   The ability to think strategically or tactically.
☆   The ability to assess and minimize risks and potential problems.
☆   The ability to work effectively in crisis or under time pressure.
☆   The ability to persuade others to your point of view.
☆   The ability to translate abstract goals into practical operating priorities.
☆   The ability to develop and implement programs, procedures or curricula.
☆   The ability to manage complex projects.
☆   The ability to plan, conduct, and document viable research.
☆   The ability to acquire needed technical skills easily ("quick study").

In emphasizing your transferable abilities to the job market, what you're really doing is proving your ability to generalize, to apply experience gained in one setting to another one. In making cabinet selections, the president doesn't focus primarily on technical skills ("Have you ever been a Secretary of State before?"). On the contrary, he's looking for desired strengths and competencies that have been amply demonstrated in other settings.

For younger networkers or anyone at the outset of a working career, the transferable abilities column poses a major problem: How do you sell your experience and past accomplishments when you aren't old enough (or working long enough) to have many? The time-honored answer is that those who don't have much experience to sell must rely primarily on the other categories in the template: they can sell their technical skills ("I just got out of school with a degree in computer science and expertise in fourth-generation computer languages") or their personal qualities—intelligence, energy, interpersonal abilities, and so on. Some younger job seekers are helped by the fact that some abilities aren't developed through life experience; instead, they stem from natural aptitude. Not everyone brings significant natural aptitude to the job market, but a gene pool will occasionally load a person with some powerful natural tools: quantitative aptitude, mathematical aptitude, creativity, critical thinking ability, logic, visual–spatial perception, and physical endurance.

A journalist once asked Greg LeMond, champion bike racer and three-time winner of the Tour de France, how to become a world-class racer. "First," said LeMond, "get yourself a set of parents with the right genes."

If you're blessed with a natural aptitude, you know it. It generally will have emerged long before you became old enough to begin work. Your main tasks, therefore, will be (1) finding a way to describe that natural aptitude succinctly and (2) convincing others that you do in fact have it. As noted on the template, most TAs are described by saying, "I have done . . . ." Aptitudes are described by saying "I'm a natural at . . . ." Frequently, a natural aptitude will not constitute the core of what you're going to sell to the working world, except perhaps in singing or musical performance. More often, aptitudes serve as enhancers of other qualities and should be described that way.

The Only Two Career-Changing Strategies

If you understand the difference between TSs and TAs, then you can see that there are only two fundamental strategies for career change. After you renounce one set of technical skills (and hence the setting in which they pertain: "I hereby 'un-become' an accountant"), you can either (1) acquire a new set of technical skills (by going back to school, taking seminars or otherwise re-educating yourself) or (2) concentrate on marketing your transferable abilities—your experience—in a new setting.

The main virtue of the first strategy is that you never lose your identity: "I used to be a CPA; now I'm a marine biologist." The rub, of course, is that you lose level: you must stop your career, go back to school, then re-emerge as a beginner. When you recast yourself in terms of your transferable abilities, you have a better chance of maintaining level (people understand that they have to pay for experience), but you lose your identity until you acquire a new one as defined by your new role. In the meantime, you're just an "ex"-something ("I'm a former CPA . . .") with a bunch of transferable abilities (the ability to organize complex data, for example) that could be put to good use in scores of different kinds of jobs.

Getting Personal

The idea of "fit," both from your point of view and your eventual employer's, starts with understanding what you have to sell—your particular mix of skills and abilities (TSs and TAs). From there on, your personal qualities will determine whether you'll enjoy a certain kind of job or work setting and whether a particular employer will be comfortable and will feel a sense of rapport with you.

Getting enough distance from yourself to develop an objective personal perspective isn't an easy task. A lot of components combine to determine your individual mix of personal qualities: your gene pool; your social/religious/economic milieu and the values and biases to which you were exposed while growing up; major life events (positive or negative); your role models; the expectations of your family, friends, peers and colleagues; your operative values; and your own unique biography. Without umpteen years of psychoanalysis, it may seem impossible to get a handle on all that makes you *you*.

For our purposes here, your personal qualities translate into a set of *preferences* concerning your type of work, work setting and co-workers. These preferences define what makes you comfortable and productive.

By *personal qualities,* we don't mean the Boy Scout virtues—kind, trustworthy, brave, obedient, cheerful; PQs are those dimensions of your character or personality that determine what motivates you, gratifies you, delights you, annoys you, terrifies you or brings out the worst in you.

Put another way, your TSs and TAs tell what you have to *sell,* and your PQs focus on what you ought to be *buying* in your next job—what you should expect and demand of any role that's truly a good fit. The point of working through the often uncomfortable process of holding a mirror up to your psyche isn't just to acquire a lot of abstract information. It's to identify job situations and potential colleagues that recognize and value your interests, style, values and preferences in thought and action. It's much easier to shop for a job if you're clear about what it will take to make you contented, challenged and vocationally well-fed.

In developing a meaningful career path, it's absolutely crucial to attend to and honor your personal values. Before you get heavily into networking or interviewing—much less decide on whether to accept any one job opportunity—it's important to ask yourself what personal values need to find expression in your work. Service to others? Creative expression? Competing and winning? Security? Friendship? Independence? Mastery? Power and control? Personal integrity? Recognition? Career advancement? Making lots of money? Balancing work, family and leisure priorities? If your work doesn't support your personal values, your problem isn't establishing a fit with an employer; it's a lack of fit with yourself.

Your PQs also are important on the "sell" side of the equation, that is, in establishing a sense of comfort in the employer. A wise old headhunter once confided, "You know, there really are only two interview questions: (1) What can you do for me? and (2) Why do you want this job, anyway?" In other words, understanding your motivation is important to an employer. It may not be as important as the value your skills and abilities represent, but no employer should want to hire someone who's temperamentally unsuited to the job—even if the person is capable of performing satisfactorily. When we use abstract words like *rapport* and *chemistry* to describe fit, we're really talking about something much more pragmatic: the employer's sense that your job-related priorities, values and motivations are in sync with his.

In seminars, I often pose a question that stymies the troops:

> Most employers will tell you they want an employee who is goal-oriented. They'll also say they want an employee who is results-oriented. What's the difference?

Give up? Think of results orientation as a psychological craving for measurable outcomes, for closure, for the bottom line. (According to one preference-measuring instrument, the Myers–Briggs Type Indicator (MBTI), about 75 percent of the people in the United States are truly results-oriented; that is, they're more interested in ends and outcomes than in means or the quality of the journey.) Any employer who operates in the private sector has got to be fundamentally concerned with outcomes, and, when hiring, will look first for evidence that an applicant shares the emphasis on getting things done.

Goal orientation is different. A goal, put simply, is something you want. Goal orientation, therefore, is a measure of what you want and how much you want it.

It's another term for motivation. In addition to a solid results orientation, almost every employer looks for an appropriately motivated employee rather than a bored, listless or indifferent employee.

Cataloging Transferable Abilities and Personal Qualities

As noted earlier in this chapter, there are a variety of approaches to trying to develop a realistic perspective on your aptitudes, abilities, personal qualities and operative values. Your local bookstore and your library stock many books that offer self-scoring profiles. All of these profiles have the virtue of forcing you to look at yourself systematically. Keep in mind, however, that anyone is allowed to try to sell anything, and many profiles' validity (Do they in fact measure what they claim to measure?) and reliability (Do they produce consistent results across a large statistical sample?) are suspect. A danger with some so-called "personality tests"—particularly the kind you find tucked into *Cosmopolitan* or *Penthouse*—is that they may compromise validity for simplicity. Be sure that the instrument you use to guide your future has been created by someone who isn't making up theory as he goes along, or hasn't been told by the magazine's editor that the test should be skewed to make people feel good.

In addition to the self-help books and proliferating self-assessment computer software packages, plenty of outside purveyors of the psyche stand ready to help you get a fix on The Real You. They're a varied lot: psychologists administering batteries of "assessment instruments" and "projective testing"; career consultants using their experience and judgment (perhaps enhanced by some time-honored interest and personal style inventories); charlatans spreading you with their own brand of processed cheese; even your favorite uncle, who seems capable of assessing your character and career prospects in five words or less.

Before you invest time and money in other forms of vocational assessment, there's one classic exercise you ought to try, to begin to acquaint yourself with yourself. As part of the vocational assessment process they work through with their clients, almost all career consultants and outplacement counselors use some variation of "The Past Accomplishments" exercise. I recommend it highly, and I suggest that you enlist the help of a family member, friend or other job seeker to provide you with some objectivity as you work through it.

In postulating what he called the "Pleasure Principle," Sigmund Freud touched on a fairly obvious psychological fact. When people experience something they find satisfying, they will—consciously and unconsciously—try to find other situations where whatever produced the pleasure can find expression again. They will, in effect, keep feeding their preferences. By feeding them, they reinforce them. People's past experiences tend to include sizable doses of what they are capable of doing (TAs!) and what they find enjoyable (PQs!).

If you take the time to look carefully at the 10 to 15 accomplishments in your adult life—whether work-related or not—that gave you the most intense satisfaction, you'll see reflected in them a veritable inventory of both your transferable abilities and your personal preferences. This apparently simplistic exercise starts with an innocuous instruction:

Jot down a brief description of 10 to 15 accomplishments in your adult life that meet two simple criteria:

1. "I did it well."
2. "I found it enjoyable or satisfying."

Accomplishments may come from work or from other activities in your life; write them down in any order as they come to mind.

Many people report some difficulty at this stage ("I can't think of anything major or important that I've done"). This complaint is a signal that they're not focusing on events that have motivated or pleased them, but rather on things that external judges would find impressive. The point here is to identify events or activities that stick in *your* mind as satisfying memories, even if they might seem trivial to someone else.

The next step is to arrange your accomplishments in priority order. My instruction for this step usually goes, "If I took all your accomplishments away from you, save one, which one—for any reason at all that's important to you—would you choose to keep?" Then, "Which would be second?" Then third, fourth, and so on.

After you've arranged your accomplishments in your own priority order, enlist your helper to "disassemble" each accomplishment into its most important factors (this exercise often is called "factoring"). First, summarize the accomplishment for your helper: describe the situation that led up to the accomplishment, the activities you performed to make it happen, and the result of your activities. Your helper should then cross-examine you in great detail about what went into this accomplishment and should take notes about the skills and abilities the cross-examination reveals. Here is a possible script:

☆ What exactly did you do to make this happen? What did you do first? What did you do next? Be specific: What did you do after that?

☆ Why did you find this activity satisfying? Did you derive greater satisfaction from the process or the outcome? What kind of accomplishment is

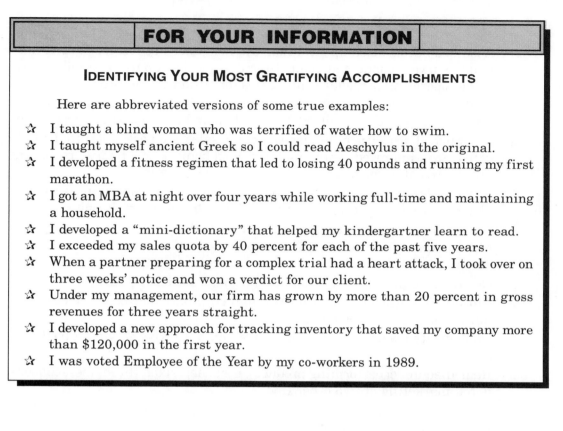

FOR YOUR INFORMATION

IDENTIFYING YOUR MOST GRATIFYING ACCOMPLISHMENTS

Here are abbreviated versions of some true examples:

☆ I taught a blind woman who was terrified of water how to swim.

☆ I taught myself ancient Greek so I could read Aeschylus in the original.

☆ I developed a fitness regimen that led to losing 40 pounds and running my first marathon.

☆ I got an MBA at night over four years while working full-time and maintaining a household.

☆ I developed a "mini-dictionary" that helped my kindergartner learn to read.

☆ I exceeded my sales quota by 40 percent for each of the past five years.

☆ When a partner preparing for a complex trial had a heart attack, I took over on three weeks' notice and won a verdict for our client.

☆ Under my management, our firm has grown by more than 20 percent in gross revenues for three years straight.

☆ I developed a new approach for tracking inventory that saved my company more than $120,000 in the first year.

☆ I was voted Employee of the Year by my co-workers in 1989.

this: Self-development? Mastery of new skills? Intellectual curiosity? Helping others? Entrepreneurial? Management? Troubleshooting? Overcoming adversity? Exceeding others' expectations? Researching? Organizing things? Organizing people? Getting measurable results? Winning over others?

☆ What does this accomplishment say about you? If it's a valid example of your abilities, what abilities does it reflect? If it reflects personal strengths or values, which ones?

As your helper lists the factors reflected in each accomplishment, encourage him to use brief phrases anchored by past-tense verbs. Let's say that you are factoring this accomplishment:

> "Took over an underperforming West Coast sales team and turned them into the company's top performers within 18 months."

Your list of factors might look like this:

☆ Assessed needs: sized up situation; interviewed sales force; conducted attitude survey; conducted competitor and market analysis; analyzed internal operating procedures and sales force support resources.

☆ Built trust among suspicious sales force: communicated candidly; encouraged feedback; admitted I needed their help; remained accessible.

☆ Established priorities: developed better sales support; recruited motivated staff; improved communication with home office; revised reporting procedures; designed/implemented incentive program.

☆ Recruited new staff: wrote job descriptions; placed ads; handled interviewing; negotiated compensation and conditions of employment.

☆ Screened and supervised consultant in installing new incentive program.

☆ Met personally with all existing customers in region; won trust of hostile major account.

☆ Coordinated activities of local and national marketing staff.

☆ Cut office overhead 35 percent through elimination of nonproductive administrative and sales staff.

☆ Implemented weekly dinner meetings and biweekly individual feedback sessions.

☆ Remedied underperforming product lines; deep-sixed three lines; consolidated marketing of two other lines.

☆ Developed new procedures for communicating with home office and other five regions, including purchasing and implementing new automated real-time order tracking system.

Get the idea? Factoring is difficult and slow at first. Its toughest lesson is to refrain from talking in abstractions and, instead, to define your past accomplishments in terms of specific, observable behaviors. Once you've factored your number-one accomplishment, move on to number two, number three, and so on, using exactly the same technique.

What you'll find immediately is that some activities repeat: "initiated new program . . . assessed needs . . . developed strategic plan . . . set priorities . . . created standards . . . coordinated activity . . . developed new approach . . . managed complex detail . . . increased profits," and so on. You'll also note that certain personal qualities keep showing up: autonomy, perseverance, taking on new challenges, creativity, or human-oriented values, for example.

According to Freud, this repetition is no accident. The point of the whole factoring process is to see what activities, abilities and personality traits seek and find expression repeatedly in the things you've done well and enjoyed.

Suppose that, among your 15 accomplishments, some form of initiative ("developed plan," "started company," "invented process," "initiated discussions") occurs 12 times. Do you think that's coincidental? Hardly. You therefore are entitled to say to a networking contact or potential employer, "I have a lot of initiative." Your past acts prove it. You also should understand that if initiative occurs 12 of 15 times, it had better be an instrumental part of your next job. If you ignore an ability or personal quality that you've used and enjoyed in the past, you're going to starve a part of you that's been well-fed in the past.

Other Self-Assessment Tools

Once you've completed the Past Accomplishments Exercise, you may feel that you have a clear enough view of your TAs and PQs to complete your self-assessment template, commit it to memory and leap right into the networking fray. If so, fine. Go to it!

In many people, however, this exercise sparks a hunger for a deeper and more objective look at themselves. That's where the other self-assessment instruments, software programs and career counselors can come in (and some of your dollars go out).

Instruments for charting personality characteristics, interest patterns and operative values are too numerous to list here (there are hundreds of them), but some of the most popular ones are essentially stereotyping tools derived from the thinking of psychoanalyst Carl Jung, who posited four fundamental personality orientations: (1) Thinker, (2) Feeler, (3) Intuitor and (4) Sensor. Jung then looked at the types of people and situations that fed or frustrated these types.

One of the oldest and most widely known of these instruments is the Myers–Briggs Type Indicator (MBTI), taken by tens of thousands of people worldwide and continually refined to become something of an industry standard. The MBTI is based on Jungian types and purports to measure personal preferences across four dimensions:

1. Style of thinking and ordering information;

2. Principles that shape the decision-making process;

3. Strength of the desire for order, control, and closure (or their opposites: spontaneity and variety);

4. Whether you draw and direct your energy from outside or inside.

Although I'm a Myers–Briggs user and fan, I can see why the instrument has its ardent critics. Actually, the problem is less with the instrument than with the overly simplistic way in which it's often interpreted. The instrument profiles a person in terms of one of 16 four-letter types that resemble license plates. I've run into a lot of people who wear those license plates around their necks like dog tags and use them to restrict—not expand—their self-understanding. The MBTI—and similar instruments—are descriptive, not prescriptive, and are best used to identify your comfort zones, not to tell you what to do with your life.

Many people ardently resent being stereotyped in any way and will stridently assert their absolute individuality. These same people, however, may need to be reminded that calling someone a genius, a team player, a dork or a dweeb also is a form of stereotyping. We all stereotype others all the time, and except when used inappropriately, stereotypes have the benefit of allowing us to think in terms of categories. Stereotypes exist because they have some utility to whoever is using them. To its credit, the MBTI is a statistically validated and value-neutral stereotyping instrument.

The Strong Interest Inventory (previously called the Strong–Campbell) frequently is used by career counselors in conjunction with the MBTI because the two tend to work hand-in-glove: the MBTI is an abstract representation of certain preferences; the Strong Interest Inventory maps how those preferences tend to express themselves in terms of degree of interest in specific occupations, activities, people and areas of knowledge.

There are many other similar instruments. Some are elegant and easy to remember; others are complex, confusing and virtually impossible to process and digest. The thing to remember about all of them is that, like mirrors, they reflect back what you project onto them. None is clairvoyant or magical. All are susceptible to some distortion. If you ever feel that the results being fed back on one of these instruments are wrong ("Gee, I never thought I was an introvert, but if the test says I am, I guess I must be one"), the instrument is wrong. Skilled career counselors generally use a variety of instruments or information-gathering approaches; they're looking for cross-validation of the reflections back from the mirror.

No instrument or battery of instruments will tell you exactly what you should do with your life, and none lists the thousands of vocational options that may be appropriate for a particular vocational profile. What the instruments can do, however, is help you identify the type of role you're best suited for, a setting where your strengths are appreciated and well-utilized, and colleagues with whom you'd enjoy working, day in and day out.

Perhaps even more to the point, the instruments often make clear what you *shouldn't do;* they describe activities, situations, or roles (or people) with which you have no affinity or interest. If this seems a backward approach to self-assessment, think of this parallel: When a doctor attempts to pinpoint what ails a patient, he usually uses a "rule-out diagnosis." Instead of trying to identify the disease imme-diately he first eliminates as many categories of illness as he can. That approach creates a much more focused universe of viable possibilities, and it significantly diminishes the risk of a misdiagnosis (or, in the job seeker's case, a misfit).

Stated another way, quantitative assessment instruments can help you be true "to thine own self" by providing generic descriptions of what motivates you and what turns you off. When it comes time to start networking, any information that reduces the amount of territory you have to explore is invaluable.

The Battle between Role and Soul

Many of us find it difficult to stay clear of jobs and activities we shouldn't do—or shouldn't even think about!—because strong external forces may be shoving us in the wrong direction. In their struggle to "know themselves," people often can't distinguish between their "soul" (the traits and preferences that define their basic temperament) and their "role" (all the other outside factors that impinge on their judgment).

What results is the classic recipe for career unrest: in an effort to please par-ents, spouses and peers, to live up to socioeconomic expectations and myths, to try to copy the successes of others, or to generally remain "above reproach," people choose careers that are strikingly at odds with their essential nature—often without knowing they're doing it. Unless we're gifted with world-class objectiv-ity, we find it hard to distinguish what we really want from what we think we ought to want, from what others tell us we should want, and from what's realistic to want. Is it any wonder that, when trying to figure ourselves out and set career objectives and priorities, we can't tell whether we're driving or being driven?

The Dark Side of the Moon

The primary thrust of this chapter has been to help you define your most mar-ketable skills, experiences, personal qualities, temperamental traits and other positive factors to attract employer interest. When both networking and inter-viewing, you must be focused, succinct and better than your competitors in high-lighting your positive features. A good self-assessment will clarify what you have to sell.

However, as long as you're completing this self-scrutiny, it behooves you to have an honest, objective look at the "dark side of the moon," that is, to confront your vulnerable soft spots, aversions, deficits and areas of rigidity or inflexibility. It's unpleasant to catalog things or situations that make you uncomfortable; it's tough to confess that you're an imperfect creature. Nonetheless, these factors are an integral part of your vocational profile, and you don't make them disappear by ignoring them.

In figuring out "what to buy" in your career—as opposed to looking solely at what you can sell—understand the difference between motivations and compensations. Motivation is positive, active energy composed of raw, primary enthusiasm. It's gasoline thrown on the fire. It's up, forward, wanting more; it's fun.

Compensations represent the flip side. They're the accommodations you make to stay away from pain and vulnerability, to circumvent your demons and shortcomings, and to incorporate your glitches and blips into a life- and work-style that don't make you miserable. When psychologists speak of someone being "well-compensated," they're not talking about making the big bucks; they're describing someone who's able to integrate his strengths and weaknesses into an operative style and a set of life choices that free him up to pursue his motivations.

A fundamental principle here is worth emphasizing: *You cannot consistently tap into the energy provided by your sources of motivation until you've first addressed those areas and issues that require compensation.*

Indeed, we have a label for people who display enormous energy directed primarily at compensation. We call them driven, and behind their backs we agree that they aren't having much fun.

Understanding your soft spots and incorporating them into the product you want to sell to employers doesn't mean that you must don a hair shirt, stake yourself out in the noonday sun and proclaim to the world, "I'm defective, unworthy and weak!" Make that approach the basis of your networking and no one in his right mind will refer you to any further contacts.

FOR YOUR INFORMATION

THINK POSITIVELY ABOUT WHO YOU ARE

Conflict-averse	becomes	Consensus builder
Loner	becomes	Works well independently
Control freak	becomes	Strong leadership profile
Disorganized	becomes	Strategic thinking visionary
Risk-averse	becomes	Risk manager
Impulsive	becomes	Spontaneous
Conformist	becomes	Team player

This chapter is talking about fit, so let's bag the idea of weak versus strong and bad versus good as unproductive. Personal qualities are neither bad nor good per se. They're simply functional or dysfunctional, depending on the context in which they emerge. A strength in one setting often is a deficit in another. A person might be labeled by a critic as "unassertive, disorganized, not detail-oriented, vague, abstract and impulsive," and by a fan as "consensus-building, flexible, not hung up on trivia, visionary, creative and spontaneous." Beauty is in the eye of the beholder.

Instead of worrying about labels, think instead about what your temperamental qualities imply in terms of the kind of role you want and could work in comfortably. When you hold a mirror of truth up to yourself, you may want to do some relabeling to make the glass half full rather than half empty. That's OK.

The idea isn't to kid yourself or paint everything with a rose-colored brush. Describe your attributes neutrally and objectively so that you can use them to determine whether a particular job is a good fit. Shy away from yourself (it's called denial) at this crucial point, and you'll get what you deserve: a job or career where you're always striving to compensate and where your motivations seem to go forever unsatisfied.

Putting It All Together: "The two-minute drill"

Let's say you've worked through a diligent, realistic self-assessment. You've cataloged your skills, abilities, hot buttons and blind spots and entered them dutifully on your template (see Table 2.1). Now, when you hear the request, "Tell me about yourself," you're armed and ready.

But all this assessment has taken place behind closed doors. You're now filled with insight and self-awareness; it's time to face the final challenge, open up the hangar doors, wheel your product profile out into the sunlight, and see whether you can articulate it succinctly and confidently to someone else. Your final step in prenetworking preparation is to pull all this information together into a short, coherent, interesting and memorable narrative, and practice delivering it calmly and confidently on demand.

A crucial step at the outset of any networking meeting is for you to give the contact enough information about you—without blathering on interminably or burying him in detail—that he can put you in perspective. You should outline and practice what many career-counselors call "the two-minute drill"—a brief introductory summary that covers level, role/function and setting, as well as your TSs, TAs and PQs. Your summary doesn't have to be confined to two minutes, but if it stretches out past five minutes, you're probably going into too much detail or sliding into a sales pitch.

In today's real world, you have to add two additional bits of information: (1) The Tale ("Why are you in the job market? Why are you making a career shift?") and (2) The Objective Statement ("What do you want to do next?"). We'll talk about these two components in Chapter 5, when we discuss the form and content of networking meetings. For the moment, it's enough to know that the job market is a skeptical, defensive and overcrowded place and that projecting a clear focus to a networking contact will involve addressing the issue of Why this, why now?

Even though it adds to the stress, let's reemphasize that your two-minute drill has to be interesting as well as succinct. This is your sound track; if you can't communicate interest in what you're presenting, no one else will be interested either. There's a common tendency among networkers to rattle off a sequential list of past jobs and hope the contact will draw all the proper inferences.

That approach is not good enough. Your summary statement should cover why you made the career decisions you did, what parts of your work you really enjoyed, and what aspects you can do without in the future. Feel free to comment on your prior decisions and explain where you were well-focused and where you should have given more weight.

But remember, if you can help it, *no negatives!* Any kind of negative sticks in the mind of the listener and dilutes the other messages being received. Keep the glass half full by avoiding negative droplets: "I flunked out." "I couldn't hack it." "I hated the place and everyone in it." "I had a problem." "They fired me." "I was asked to leave."

Almost anything can be expressed in a value-neutral way: "I took a semester off." "We had different ways of doing things." "It seemed like the thing to do at the time." "I learned that I work more comfortably in less-structured settings." "It was clear to me that my long-term career prospects would be better served in another setting."

Let's have a look at a couple of two-minute drills. One has been concocted, the other is a lightly disguised true-life tale. Listen first to the hypothetical conventional job searcher:

> Maybe the best place to start is to give you a quick thumbnail sketch of my background. I'm presently Vice President of Human Resources for AJAKS, a $1 billion manufacturer of computer peripherals. I've had this job for about four years, although I've been with the company for eight.
>
> I came up through the comp and benefits side of the house, and along the way I picked up a lot of expertise in pension planning and administration, ESOPs, executive incentive plans, and other approaches to financial benefits. They had me doing technical and executive recruiting for a while, and I learned how to write a decent job spec and interview well, but I was pleased when I got promoted to supervise that function—along with all recruiting,

manpower and succession planning—in addition to handling the restructuring of the company's approach to comp at all levels, rather than having to do it myself every day.

Just before I got promoted, there was a successful campaign to unionize our manufacturing floor staff, and we had a very hairy six months. I had to learn a lot about labor relations and employee relations on the fly because, at the same time, I was called on to troubleshoot some crises that arose when we centralized our whole HR function after acquiring two other companies. I found I had a real flair for labor relations, and I got a reputation—even among the union reps—for being reasonable and adaptable, and that has stood me in good stead.

When my predecessor retired, they gave me the VP job on an interim basis to see if I could pick up all the "soft side" HR stuff . . . you know, organizational development, training, management development, team building, corporate culture and strategic HR planning. I think the people who'd branded me as sort of a comp-and-benefit techie were pleasantly surprised at some of the programs I initiated and implemented. I was pretty aggressive in working to develop better communications—formal and informal—in the organization, and I even got the union to buy into some performance evaluation approaches you would have expected them to resist.

I've really been enjoying myself in this job; it's a long way from Eagle River, Wisconsin, and a bachelor's degree in History from the University of Wisconsin at Stevens Point. I might note that my early career was spent as an abstractor with a title company in Milwaukee. They were really nice folks, but I learned real fast that highly repetitive, quantitative stuff was not nearly as interesting to me as roles that focused on people rather than data.

The company sponsored me in an Executive MBA program several years ago, and I've found that having a broader knowledge of operations, marketing and finance really has helped me manage my function. It didn't make me want to flip over into general management, though. I really want to stay in this kind of work. However, a change may be in the offing. A large French conglomerate is poised to buy us out, and they have a history of replacing senior staff managers with their own people. I think it may be prudent to step out before I'm pushed, and I was hoping—even in a recession—to catch on with another rapid-growth manufacturing company—union or not—to head up their HR function.

It's all in there: level, role, function, setting, skills, abilities, temperament, what he liked most (and liked less), educational background, reason for being in the job market, statement of what he wants to do next.

Career shifters will look at this tight, lucid narrative and say, "Yeah, but this guy has it easy! He's a nice, easy-to-define product with a nice, linear career path. What do you say if you're going to leave what you were doing before or if your prior career path has all sorts of bizarre twists and turns?"

Calvin's Story

When you have a lot of explaining to do or if your future focus isn't entirely clear, the best course is to develop a chronological narrative that explains, step-by-step, how you got where you are now. In such a narrative, it's particularly important to explain the reasons for your job transitions, as Calvin did in the following true-life example:

I was born and raised in the South Bronx, the youngest of five kids. We didn't have too much, so all us kids got self-reliant pretty early. I was sort of the "angry young man" in high school, but that was getting me nowhere, so I decided to get some credentials that I could use to ensure myself some economic security. I went to the University of Kansas and got a degree in mechanical engineering. My grades were very good, and I got hired straight out of school by ARAMCO, who sent me to Saudi Arabia to work on building new refineries. I found I was a natural at engineering project management, and, by age 26, I was the project manager on a $60 million refinery construction project, managing people from a variety of cultures, disciplines and backgrounds. I proved good at troubleshooting complex construction problems and at keeping a tight rein on costs, which won me some strokes with senior management.

I was getting pretty removed from the U.S. mainstream, though, and when a $200 million plant I was going to head didn't get built because of the Mideast economic climate, I decided to change course. I came back to the United States, got into Harvard Law School, and did well. I got recruited by the Dallas office of the country's largest law firm, Bigg, Large & Humongous, where I was involved in large lawsuits, defending our clients—who generally were Fortune 100 corporations—in hostile takeover attempts and proxy fights. By doing this for a couple of years, I learned a lot about business deals and finance, but I could see being involved in litigation wasn't where I wanted to take my life. So I accepted an offer to be a corporate lawyer—not a litigator—with a large Houston company, Strong & Hearte Inc., where I've been involved in general corporate practice and—the part I like best—transactional work, that is, doing deals.

What has become clear to me in doing this is that I like business more as a participant than as a specialized consultant. I've come to realize that I'm both autonomous and entrepreneurial by nature, and that I'm probably never going to be as comfortable in a large, structured setting as I am in "doing my own thing." So it looks like I'm in the middle of making another major shift. I value what I've learned as a corporate lawyer, but I've been talking with a variety of possible co-venturers about getting involved in one or more entrepreneurial activities—perhaps venture capital, perhaps starting a Small Business Investment Company (a SBIC, as they're called), marketing construction project management for a minority-owned firm or doing some real estate development. I'll never be better situated to take this kind of risk, so I've decided that my "credentialing" years are through and that it's time to build my career around the kinds of roles and activities I like the best. Whether I end up with the label of lawyer in my next role depends on whom I hook up with and what their needs are.

Beyond the fact that this two-minute drill gets a quart of information into a pint pot of time, you should note something more: as is the case with many career changers, it isn't possible for Calvin to put a firm, clear label on the product he's selling. What he ends up doing next is going to depend on the people he meets while networking, where they send him, and what ideas they come up with.

Calvin is hard to pigeonhole, and one of the initial priorities in his networking will be to get the information that will help him rule out unproductive directions and unrealistic expectations. He'll become better focused as he goes along, his two-minute drill will tighten accordingly, and he'll feel less that he's at the mercy of a job market he can't control.

Calvin's two-minute drill didn't just magically pop out as a coherent narrative. He worked through an intense career reappraisal with a career consultant. He took the time, perhaps for the first time in his life, to put his past choices in perspective and examine what they could tell him about his future. He outlined the two-minute drill and practiced it with his wife and friends. He weathered a couple of sessions in front of a video camera in which he first felt "as if I had rented lips." He got good. His story and motives became clear. He became confident that he could recast and refocus his self-description on the fly and respond skillfully to bolts out of the blue.

True, Calvin has a lot of skills, experience and personal strengths to sell. But without the ability to synthesize his strengths and communicate them in a way that makes sense, Calvin would be unable to make the splash he deserves in the job market. So it is with all fledgling networkers, whether they're going to run a conventional job search or shift gears and direction. Every networker reports that the process gets easier as you go along, that you become more focused and relaxed the more you do it. But you have to start with a core of insight, then develop the ability to communicate that insight. So, before forging ahead into matters of technique, do some valuable homework. Get to know thyself.

". . . interview . . . interview . . . interview . . ."

3

Who Should I See and Why Will They See Me?

I f you've begun to contemplate how you'll identify potential networking contacts, chances are you're also fretting about another issue. You're probably
thinking: "This whole networking technique is going to require that I write
or call a bunch of people who don't know me and who owe me nothing. I have
to ask them to give me some of their precious time and almost assume that they're
going to do it. Why in the world would they do that? In today's business world,
where time is money, what incentive does anyone have to give time away?"

Good questions.

Radio Station WITN-FM

The job market has its share of altruists and charitable souls, but they're not numerous enough to explain networking's long success as the premier job search technique. Most theories of job search motivation are broadcast on the frequency of WITN-FM: "What's In This Networking—For Me?"

To understand why your "bunch of people" are going to give you one of their scarcest resources, their time, consider the benefits that will accrue to them. You *know* your close friends will see you. They've got to; that's the essence of friendship. If they value the relationship, they'll rise to the occasion. (One of the fastest ways to distinguish a real friend from an acquaintance or a fair-weather friend is to ask the friend to expend time and effort on the relationship. If he runs for the hills or proffers an empty sleeve, you'll know the relationship was insubstantial.)

Given that real friendship is a two-way street, it follows that you'll stand willing to help your friends when they have a need. It's possible to start your networking efforts cold, with people you've never met (headhunters do it all the time), but it's easier and less daunting to start the process with the people you know best and trust most. Your path outward from there will be much smoother.

When you've cultivated all the contacts you know and have begun to reach out to people you don't know (and who owe you nothing), a different, more pragmatic set of WITN-FM incentives kicks in. A lot of people will agree to network with you as a favor to the person who referred you to them. Once that favor has been conferred, they know that two people have an unspoken obligation to return the favor: (1) you and (2) the person who referred you. Most of us carry an informal but indelible tally of whom we've granted favors to (who "owes us one") and who has granted favors to us.

The business world is lubricated by what I call a "pseudo-economy of reciprocal favors" in which the Favor is the informal—but very powerful—unit of exchange. The Favor Market, in fact, is a lot like the stock market: it has puts, calls, warrants, options, bartering and insider information.

The Favor Market isn't confined to job search-related networking; it operates as the vehicle for daily, informal swapping of information. By tapping into it for career development and job search purposes, you're utilizing a practical and long-standing mechanism. Networking works particularly well as a job search facilitation tool, however, because the information provided can often lead to an immediate and tangible outcome: a job for someone who needs it. The gratitude of the job seeker—and the sense of obligation to somehow return the favor—is then enormous.

If you provide someone with a tidbit of information that leads to happy employment, you've probably created more than a reservoir of goodwill. The response signal on WITN-FM? Probably a lifetime supply of favors from the lucky recipient of your help.

People will expend precious time to network with you for another practical reason: They want to pick your brain. Networking isn't a one-way street; it's an exchange of informal, juicy and potentially valuable information. Within the dictates of propriety and confidentiality, therefore, be prepared to offer up some insights about whom you've networked with, what you've learned so far about trends in their industries, why your old employer just laid off 350 technicians, whom you know in the mayor's office who might listen to your contact's concern about a zoning problem and, perhaps, how to program a four-head VCR.

Soft Doesn't Mean Fuzzy

The most potent reasons why people will see you are grounded in the workings of human nature, not in the realities of the outside world. These "soft" motives may not be readily visible, but you can rely on them as universal and reliable forces.

In this vein, you must understand that experts, whether true or self-proclaimed, love to share their expertise. All of us like to be thought of as wise; each of us savors the recognition and visibility that are reflected in a flattering referral: "Jack says you know more about marketing in Central America than anyone he knows, and that you are the best contact he can imagine to explore the feasibility of selling my product line there."

Come prepared to listen and give the networking contact plenty of air time. This advice conflicts with one of the other fundamental purposes of networking—to gain market exposure and to be able to talk about yourself in a way that conveys *your* expertise (and your transferable abilities and personal qualities). The balance between sending and receiving often is thrown off by the static that begins when a networker grabs the mike, hogs all the air time and talks the contact's ear off about himself. A programming note: This kind of script won't win you friends or enthusiastic referrals.

The second point to remember is: Before you go into a networking meeting, be sure you know what your expert is expert at. The following type of exchange is all too common:

Networker: Mr. Jones, I was talking with your acquaintance, Bruce Smith, the other day, and he said you'd be a really great person to network with . . . so . . . ah . . . that's why I'm calling.

FOR YOUR INFORMATION

NETWORKING IS A TWO-WAY STREET

A man once asked me to attend a networking meeting. He was in town for only one day and had heard that I knew "what was going on in human resources in Philly."

We agreed to meet at 5:00, and I explained that we absolutely had to wrap up by 5:40. He arrived promptly and immediately launched into a lecture about the human resource function in large corporations. He talked comfortably and articulately, never pausing for a moment to let me share my own wisdom. After looking at my watch a few times, I began straightening the papers on my desk at 5:30. He kept talking. I began stuffing papers into my briefcase, and at 5:40 I stood up. He stood up . . . and kept talking. I shrugged and started down the hall, and he matched me pace for pace . . . and kept talking.

Finally, in the elevator lobby, I waved my hands semaphore style in his face and screeched, "Stop! What do you think you're doing? You've run about four red lights. You've lectured me about stuff I already know. You never asked for my opinion about anything! What is this, the first networking meeting you've ever done?!" His eyes opened wide: "How did you know?"

Contact: Why did Bruce mention me? In what way did he think I'd be able to help you?
Networker: I dunno. He just said you'd be a good person to talk to.

This opening is a real recipe for groping around blindly, wasting the networker's time and fostering the notion that you're unfocused and unprepared. Make sure you know why you've been referred to any particular contact, and take the time to prepare focused questions. At the very least, think seriously about the kinds of information or areas of knowledge you'll bring up in the networking meeting.

Perhaps the most potent and predictable reason that contacts will agree to meet with you is that people like to help people. In fact, most people find it hard to turn down requests for assistance. Exactly why they respond positively to requests for help is a matter we can leave to psychologists. Does a strain of pure altruism run through us all? Does rendering help create a dominant–subordinate relationship that gratifies our need for control? Is empowerment a universal human trait? Do we all subconsciously hope that help given is like cosmic money-in-the-bank—a moral savings account that we'll be able to draw on if we ever need help ourselves? In today's economy, do those who have jobs wonder whether a need to network might be waiting in their own future?

Who knows? The fact remains that most people will respond favorably to a request for help. A word of caution, however: it's not hard to turn off that impulse by:

☆ Asking for too much help: "Could you lend me $50,000, put me up in your spare bedroom and make sense out of my life for me?"

☆ Asking for too much time: "Could you spare half a day for me on Tuesday?"

☆ Whining, wheedling or making presumptuous demands: "Jack says you're the best person to network with, so I'll call Tuesday at 2:30 to schedule a meeting in the early afternoon of next Monday. I'll need you to review my resume and provide me with sound advice on available job openings."

The bottom line is: If you mind your manners and show an elementary understanding of human nature, most people will see you. That leaves you with no excuse for backing away from the networking process. Let's get a list together and start to work through it.

Whom Should You Talk To?

Advising you to network with every living, breathing human you can get to talk to you probably isn't helpful advice, even though it may turn out to be true. Networking is a numbers game: The more people you see, the more chances you have to learn the juicy tidbits of information you need, and the greater your market exposure. It's that simple.

But what's simple isn't always easy. Systematic networking is time-consuming. When your networking efforts gather momentum and the number of new contacts multiplies geometrically, your greatest problem will be trying to find enough time to contact them all, return phone calls, schedule meetings, attend those meetings, and make follow-up calls while continuing to expand your network. Some order or priority has to be imposed. Whom should you see first, whom do you relegate to second and when and how do you reach out to scores of low-probability contacts?

FOR YOUR INFORMATION

EVERYONE IS A POTENTIAL ANTENNA

Networkers—particularly those in technical disciplines—tend to assume that the only useful people are those in the same industry. Your contract list should certainly include colleagues, but remember that the purpose of networking is to get exposure as well as information. Don't confine your network to contacts in your profession.

In Chapter 1, we discussed the four distinct categories of networks that most of us have: (1) Personal, (2) Professional, (3) Organizational and (4) Opportunistic (Community Affiliations). To develop your initial contact lists, systematically think through your networks in each of these four categories. When you first do this, go fast; brainstorm the process. Unless phone numbers and addresses come readily to mind, skip them for the moment. Don't rule anyone out, even if you think, "Ah, Herman's an uninformed boob. He doesn't know anything and he'll never know anything." At this stage, be inclusive! Set your priorities later.

Next, using the models in Figures 3.1 through 3.4, develop worksheets that identify your resources in the four categories. Try to enter at least two names for each fill-in, if only to demonstrate to yourself the astonishing breadth of day-to-day interpersonal contacts that most of us have and never think about.

If you don't divide your thinking into these categories, you're likely to experience a common list-making phenomenon: Mind-lock. The moment you're confronted with blank sheets of paper, your conscious mind throws a few circuit-breakers and it too goes blank. You squeeze your eyes shut, tense your stomach muscles and push yourself to "think up" names.

The first time you work on your list, you'll be exhausted after an hour of pushing—and you'll find that you have 37 names written on your paper. (I don't know why it's 37, but it always is.) Later, after you've cooled down and had a couple of tall, cold de-inhibitors, gates will open and your list will swell to 73—or thereabouts. You'll say to yourself, "That's it. That's everyone I know. I'm done."

Just as you drop off to sleep that night, the relaxation of your daily defense and information-screening mechanisms will allow a whole lot of names to pop into your mind. You swear to yourself that you'll remember them in the morning, but the names will be no more remembered than the dreams you have that night. For that reason, it's very useful during list making to keep several pad-and-pencil units around: by your bed, by the refrigerator, in the bathroom and on one of those suction-cup stick-ups on the windshield of your car. When recall is sounded, you want to be ready.

Establishing Priorities: The three Ps

Let's say your straining and scribbling has given you the names of 137 people whom you know at least well enough to say "Hi" to. Intimacy isn't important; you need only enough familiarity to provide license for a friendly, low-key call. You've consulted your holiday card list, wended your way through your high school and college yearbooks, consulted professional directories, reviewed your business correspondence for the past year, gone over the stubs in your checkbook and reviewed your phone log and daily planner.

Rewrite the names neatly on your listing sheets (Figures 3.1–3.4), this time with phone numbers and, perhaps, addresses. If you have a computer, key in all the information on each name on your listing sheets, to develop a tracking database (see Chapter 9). Alternately, buy a little metal-box file and create a 3 × 5 index card for each name.

Do you then start alphabetically with the A names and keep wading until you reach Z? Is there some sensible method for assigning priorities and deciding which contacts to call first?

As a rough rule-of-thumb, think of three Ps: (1) *Proximity,* (2) *Perspective* and (3) *Power.* Start by seeing the people who are "proximate" to you: the people you know best, trust most and feel most comfortable with. Practicing and refining your two-minute drill will be far easier when the stakes are low and the lubrication of friendship is abundant.

Heed two warnings here:

1. Your friends may take it too easy on you. They may be disinclined to really put you through your paces or to insist that you be clear, focused and succinct. Tell them at the beginning of the meeting that one of the services they can provide is to act as an objective audience and help you to refine and clarify your self-presentation as needed.

2. Your friends know you only one way. They may have an incomplete or significantly distorted view of who you are, what you do and what you want to do next. Take steps to make sure they hear and understand your product

Figure 3.1   Personal Relationships Networking Worksheet

1. List members of your immediate family and as many relatives as possible:

   _____

   _____

   _____

2. List at least 5 of your closest friends (list 10 to 15 if possible): _____

   _____

   _____

3. List the names of 3 neighbors: _____

   _____

4. My doctor(s) is: _____

5. My lawyer(s) is: _____

6. My accountant is: _____

7. My personal banker and/or trust officer is: _____

8. My insurance agent is: _____

9. My broker(s) is: _____

10. My auto mechanic is: _____

11. My minister, priest or rabbi is: _____

12. My psychologist or psychiatrist is: _____

13. List at least 5 college roommates, drinking buddies, or friends: _____

    _____

    _____

14. List 5 people you haven't been in touch with for over 5 years: _____

    _____

    _____

15. List 10 people you know from your church or synagogue, social clubs, country clubs, school/parent groups or fraternal organizations (*not* professional associations):

    _____

    _____

    _____

    _____

Figure 3.2   Professional Relationships Networking Worksheet

1. List 5 colleagues at work with whom you work closely (list 10 to 15 if possible):

    _____

    _____

2. List 5 other people at work whom you know well enough to chat with: _____

    _____

    _____

3. List the 10 colleagues in other organizations you are most often in contact with:

    _____

    _____

    _____

    _____

4. List the names of your 5 best customers or clients: _____

    _____

    _____

5. My company's lawyer or law firm is: _____

6. My company's accountant or accounting firm is: _____

7. My company's commercial banker and investment banker are: _____

    _____

8. My company's management consultant(s) is: _____

9. My company's lobbyist(s) or regulator(s) is: _____

10. My 5 most respected competitors (who know me) are: _____

    _____

    _____

11. I often have lunch at the club or local lunch hangout with: _____

    _____

12. List 5 significant investors or co-venturers in your business or ventures: _____

    _____

    _____

13. I belong to the following professional organizations or associations: _____

    _____

    _____

    [I can get a membership list of these organizations by calling or writing: _____]

Figure 3.3   Organizational and Community Associations Networking Worksheet

1. I serve on the Board of Directors or Trustees of: _____
   _____

   [Attach the list of directors of each organization to the back of this sheet.]

2. I am a member of the following organizations: _____
   _____
   _____
   _____
   _____

3. I can get the membership list of each of these groups by calling or writing: _____
   _____
   _____
   _____
   _____

4. List 3 fundraisers or development people you know: _____
   _____
   _____
   _____

5. List every organization for which you have done any volunteer work: _____
   _____
   _____
   _____
   _____
   _____
   _____
   _____
   _____

Figure 3.4   Avenues of Opportunity Worksheet

1. I subscribe to the following magazines, newspapers and periodicals: _____

   _____

   _____

2. To broaden my information base, I *could* subscribe to the following: _____

   _____

   _____

3. The 3 ways in which I most frequently meet new acquaintances are: _____

   _____

   _____

4. Five ways in which I *could* meet new acquaintances are: _____

   _____

   _____

   _____

   _____

5. The reason I have not chosen to use these ways before is: _____

   _____

6. This reason is no longer valid (at least during my job search) because: _____

   _____

7. The 5 most striking or outrageous coincidences that have occurred to me in the past 2 years are:

   _____

   _____

   _____

   _____

8. I could get more visibility by: _____

   _____

9. Two examples of "what goes around comes around" that have occurred to me in the past 2 years

   are: _____

   _____

10. The ONE reason I must be more active in creating opportunities to meet others is: _____

   _____

profile and job search objectives. Be gently insistent, as this networker was with his friend:

Networker: Barbara? Hi, this is Mel. You may have heard that I've left the bank and am running a job search. I'm trying to get up to speed with this whole "networking" trick, and I was wondering if I might drop in on you at the office for a short meeting.

Friend: Are you kidding me, Mel? You don't have to do that. I've known you for years! Hey, just send me a few copies of your resume and I'll keep my eyes and ears peeled for senior lending positions. We don't have to sit down and belabor the obvious.

Networker: I really appreciate your reaction, Barbara, but let me lean on you to get together, if we can. First of all, I'm making a shift into the development of new kinds of financial products, and the way you think of me probably isn't accurate anymore. Second, I haven't had to run a job search in 12 years, and the whole process makes me anxious. I want to be sure that I'm clearly explaining my background and what I want next. It would be a great favor if you would let me practice my presentation, give me honest feedback and *then* perhaps steer me to some contacts I don't have. I know this sounds a bit stiff and structured, Barb, but it really would be the most helpful thing I can imagine right now.

As you schedule your first 10 to 12 networking meetings, understand that your fundamental purpose is to get practice. Don't expect a whole lot of content; just aim to get your presentation up to a comfortable level. (You'll get content anyway; in fact, you might be pleasantly surprised at how well these early meetings go.) As you start networking, warm up on your most tolerant contacts—or at least on those who represent no great loss if you should happen to botch the meeting.

Before you start making calls, rate each name on your list as an A, B, C or D. A's will be your most valuable potential sources of information or help—your trump cards or heavy hitters; those who owe you major favors. At the other end are the Ds, including your idiot cousin Myron. Bs may be people you haven't talked to in a long time; Cs may be social acquaintances who like you but haven't a clue about what you do for a living. Devise some criteria for systematically categorizing your contacts, and continue to rank new names that way as they come in.

When you start the actual networking process (with your Proximate contacts), you can begin working down some of your C and D contacts. Some of these names may not be worth the effort of a scheduled, face-to-face meeting, but it won't hurt to get the word out of them and see whether you can create some antennas.

Practice your two-minute drill on them. Try some variations on the theme. Remember what countless networkers before you have learned: your haircutter—a C contact—knows an amazing amount of gossip that may be of incredible value to you.

Once you've warmed up on your Proximate leads, start seeking out your *Perspective* contacts—the ones who know a lot, are themselves well-connected, have been around the industry for years, "have seen 'em come and seen 'em go" and regard themselves—and are regarded by others—as authorities, focal points or "walking encyclopedias." These contacts include some citizens who know the political ropes and can help you distinguish the "straight skinny" from the sanitized information put out for public consumption.

War Story: Politics as usual

A major city was creating a new authority to develop and run a high-profile cultural arts zone, and the search for an executive director had been given to a respected local headhunter. The head of a local nonprofit organization, let's call him Charlie, saw the job specification and was thrilled: point-for-point, he was an utterly perfect fit. TSs, TAs, PQs—the works!—all looked like they had been pirated from his resume. How could he not get this wonderful job? The headhunter, however, knew things that he wasn't at liberty to divulge. The position was a prize political plum, and a powerful figure in state politics was using his clout to "wire" the job for a friend. Connections, not merit, would be the deciding issue.

Charlie sailed through the initial screening interview like an America's Cup champion, and his spirits soared. He told close friends of his plans to resign his present position. The headhunter, a compassionate sort, finally whispered into the ear of Charlie's long-time mentor, suggesting that he have a gentle "reality conference" with Charlie over lunch.

"Charlie, how strongly would you rate your connections in government?" asked the mentor.

"Well," said Charlie, "I've worked effectively with a broad variety of governmental agencies and constituencies. I know my way around."

"Not my point," said the mentor. "Are you personally acquainted with God?"

"No," laughed Charlie.

"Do you know what *'Que sera, sera'* means?"

"Sure," said Charlie. "What will be, will be."

"Well," said the mentor, "you've already impressed a lot of people on this search, Charlie, and that will stand you in good stead later. But, Charlie, as for your chances of getting this job, *que sera* will not *sera,* if you catch my drift."

Your Perspective contacts are the wise people whose primary benefit is to give you good advice and sage judgment. They can summarize industry trends, give you behind-the-scenes glimpses, and distinguish the real movers and shakers from the phonies. Equally important, they can evaluate your past, present and future career choices (within appropriate limits, of course) and help you refine your thinking and terminology; highlight which of your past accomplishments will carry weight with employers in a new area or industry; and put a new spin on your past career moves. They also can warn you away from jobs, industries, objectives or goals that are unrealistic, unpromising or more unattractive than they may seem.

When chatting with your Perspective contacts, encourage their complete candor. Be frank, and ask for frankness in response. There is a fine line between being highly motivated and being so "up" that others are reluctant to rain on your parade or puncture your balloon by telling you the truth. If you communicate that your zeal will cause you to turn a deaf ear to "negative waves," your contacts may let you keep dancing out there in la-la land—to your eventual regret.

If one of your contacts says that what you so dearly want is "clearly out of the question," don't accept that advice at face value and recast your dreams and aspirations. There's no requirement to suspend your judgment or ignore your research when you're networking. If someone is lukewarm about the desirability or feasibility of a proposed job choice, ask detailed questions about why your planned course seems unpromising. In probing his thinking (not just his conclusions), you may discover these three valuable lessons:

1. You miscommunicated; the person didn't understand your objectives.
2. Certain arguments or reservations will reappear for rebuttal as you pursue your objective.
3. You may have to acquire new skills or experience in order to be taken seriously in your new career role.

Generally speaking, it's best to reserve your *Power* contacts until you know exactly what to ask for and how to ask for it. Power contacts are people who have the formal or informal authority to get things done: to open doors, call in favors, get you pulled through the screen and make sure you're seen by the right people. If, early in your networking efforts, you call on these people for help and don't know what kind of help to ask for, you run the risk of turning them off, dissipating the momentum they can provide and losing the benefit of their clout forever.

"It isn't my job to make sense out of your life," the president of a major pharmaceutical company told a networker (a senior manager in a related industry), when he called to ask for a meeting. "I'm not interested in helping you objectify your objectives or prioritize your priorities. When you can tell me precisely whom you want to see and why you want to see them, call me back and we'll sit down to talk. Hold up your end, and I'll be happy to open some doors. Waste my time, and you'll wish you hadn't."

There will be people who bridge all three Ps. You probably have some wise and powerful friends. The point is, networking contacts come in all denominations, and if you spend all the big bills first and don't hit paydirt, you'll have nothing but small change left later on. For most job seekers—and certainly for the vast majority of career changers—the initial phase of networking is one of gaining confidence, focus, goal clarity and as much information as you can about where the big game are to be found. It's a time for learning new terms of art and shoptalk, for ruling out unrealistic ideas and mistaken assumptions. It is, to mix a metaphor, more likely to be a time of sowing than a time of reaping. Don't be impatient, don't go for the fast hit, don't indulge in rescue fantasies. If a heavy hitter steps in and decides to champion your cause, great! But understand that such luck is the exception, not the norm.

As you progress in your networking, the task of keeping track of all the old contacts, new contacts, call-backs and follow-ups will become daunting. The easy leverage of calling on friends will give way to second-, third- and fourth-tier networking where no prior relationship eases the way. You'll be rowing the boat entirely by yourself. If you impress, you'll get more referrals to more contacts who have Perspective, Power or both.

If you fail to carry your weight, you'll know it soon enough. The meetings will be short and perfunctory, and the stream of new names—whether As, Bs, Cs or Ds—will shrink to a trickle. When this happens, a lot of frustrated networkers blame the system, not themselves. Often, the problem is inadequate preparation, pure and simple. Effective networkers know that you can't make it up as you go along or wing it in each and every meeting. As the process goes on, the stakes get higher and the contacts are more valuable. Plan on spending as much time keeping your lists in order as you did creating them in the first place.

As you build your initial networking list and prioritize it, remember one networker's description of the whole process: "No, no, no, no, no, yes, no, no, no, no, yes, yes, no, no, no, yes, yes, yes, no, no, yes???, no, no, no, no, no, no, no. . . . YES!"

As with most challenges in life, it's the last word that counts.

"Hi, Jack's the name, sales is my game, check it out . . . Hi, Jack's the name, sales is my game, check it out . . . Hi, Jack's the name . . ."

4

Into the Fray: Asking for Meetings

I t's time to begin. You're ready to start asking others for help. That thought drives a lot of job seekers crazy, particularly high achievers who have well-developed egos. You're about to hit on a whole card file of people for favors, to become beholden to most of them, and to risk being scoffed at or patronized. You might even have to admit that you're not in complete control of your own destiny.

The introverts among us—by one measure, we're about 30 percent of the U.S. population—don't particularly relish meeting strangers. Deep down in our psyche may be a notion that the world should come to us, seeking out our many virtues. To this population, networking is no different than other interpersonal "grip and grin" activities, such as fund-raising, greeting a political crowd, working the room at the Chamber of Commerce breakfast or selling vinyl siding to widows.

The primary reason most of us dislike asking others for help is that it seems to involve giving power away—and who ever gets enough to give some away? The answer is: We all do. Throughout history, many effective statesmen—Ben Franklin comes to mind—knew and practiced a very basic principle of human nature: The more power you give away, the more you have. It's when you try to *take* power that people have an incentive to give you a tough time.

Keeping It All in Perspective

The key to networking success—and to avoiding a major case of networking negativism—lies in understanding that you aren't asking for a giant favor that creates a giant debt and gives others leverage over you. On the contrary, skillful networking is low-key, low-intensity, low-stakes, low-demand and low-risk—to both parties. You're subtly empowering the other party while not asking for much in return. That's an irresistible bargain for most people.

FOR YOUR INFORMATION

A NEAT PARLOR TRICK FOR JOB SEEKERS

Whether you are networking, asking directions or trying to get a clerk's attention, try starting a conversation with this simple phrase: "Hi. I wonder if I could have a little help." This opening will "freeze" the transaction momentarily, and the other person will listen more attentively to whatever you say next. Your approach gets this response because:

1. You've been friendly.
2. You've been direct.
3. You've already provided assurance that you won't ask for too much.
4. The person doesn't know what you want.

At the end of every such conversation, be sure to thank the person for helping, particularly if you expect other interactions to follow.

Behind every request for a networking meeting, whether it's with friends, business contacts or some member of the Great and Powerful, is a simple but essential bargain. We can paraphrase it this way:

> If you will give me an extremely miniscule portion of your precious time and wondrous expertise, I will guarantee you the satisfaction of having helped another human being—and of having created some small measure of indebtedness on my part.

You won't actually say it that way, but this is the underlying contract of a properly handled networking request. The bargain is pretty hard for most people to resist. The trick is to deliver on your promise without overworking the contact's genuine but limited willingness to help. We'll show you how to do that later.

What Are You Asking For?

Your contacts' willingness to help you will depend in large measure on how your requests are couched. Networking requests are alarming when:

☆ They ask for too much time ("Could you review my entire career reappraisal process with me?").

☆ They ask for too much help ("I wonder if you would be good enough to tell me what to do with my life.").

☆ They are expressed in such lofty, abstract or highfalutin' language that the contact is bewildered or daunted ("I wonder if we might schedule an informational interview in which we would prioritize my career development and job search objectives and discuss various viable vocational alternatives in light of existing economic and vocational realities.").

☆ They are unpleasantly pushy or involve a bald-faced lie ("I'll call you Thursday at 2:00 to schedule a meeting. We'll only need 10 minutes.").

Keep your requests for help brief, conversational and low-key. Be sincere in your use of words that emphasize the informality and relative brevity of the networking encounter. Ask "if we might get together for a brief chat" or "if we could meet for a few minutes so that I might get your thoughts and opinions about some job search ideas I've been mulling over." Ask "if I might drop in on you at work for a few minutes and pick your brain." Tell someone, "I'd be grateful if I could get your advice on how to get some exposure in the Widget market." In short, keep it light!

You can trigger just as much suspicion by asking for too little time as by asking for too much, particularly among people who are experienced in networking. Many reputed job search experts say to ask for a 20-minute networking meeting. Unless your sole purpose is to fling a lot of verbiage in the contact's face and bolt out of the room without any thoughtful discussion, you can't do a decent networking meeting in 20 minutes. It takes that long just to get warmed up, recite your two-minute drill and respond to the contact's questions about your background, motives, objectives and reason for being in the job market. A request for a 20-minute meeting, therefore, is naive, insincere or a misrepresentation of how much of the contact's time you really intend to use.

If both parties are focused and experienced networkers and are determined to cut to the chase with a minimum of small talk and extraneous meandering, a reasonably effective networking meeting can be started, warmed up, played out and completed in 40 to 45 minutes; but that's really moving along. The average networking meeting lasts about an hour, and you shouldn't let it go longer unless the contact sends out explicit signals that he wants it to continue. A 90-minute meeting is a long meeting. The possibilities are: a lot of useful information is being exchanged; both of you are really enjoying yourselves; you've gotten off on an unrelated topic; or one or the other of you is lecturing, pontificating or going into enormous detail. If a meeting runs long for good reasons, it isn't necessarily bad; but be careful to keep tabs on why it's running long. If you detect yawns, time checks, drumming fingers, doodling or other evidence of distraction, cut to the closing credits—*fast*.

How Much Should You Be in Someone's Face?

It's axiomatic in networking that you should try to get face-to-face meetings with contacts whenever possible. Body-language experts agree that more than half of all the "message content" in an interpersonal transaction is conveyed nonverbally. Confidence, credibility and authority can be communicated without a word being spoken. An image of a face leaves a more vivid memory trace than a letter or a voice on the phone. Whenever possible, meet people in person.

How closely should you live by the "I'd kill to get a face-to-face meeting" principle? If a potential contact suggests that you two "network by phone," try to change her mind. You might say, "It would probably work best if we could sit down together, Sandra, but if your schedule can't squeeze that in, so be it; I'll be grateful for your help any way I can get it." You may get the meeting if you keep pressing and don't take no for an answer, but wear your lead BVDs because you're probably going to get roasted. You not only hurt yourself if you come on like an snake-oil peddler, but you spoil it for anyone else who may ever want to network with this contact.

What about Lunch?

It's tempting to use business lunches for networking, particularly if you're employed, don't have much free time to schedule meetings and/or have to be fairly discreet when choosing where and how you get job market exposure. You can meet a variety of people over lunch without raising suspicion if your boss happens by, but you'll also gain a lot of weight and strain your budget to the breaking point.

Any networking meeting is a favor to you, so you're usually obligated to repay that favor by offering to buy lunch. Polite folks might resist, and in some cases you may get away with going Dutch. But be prepared to reach for the check. If you do a lot of networking—and you should!—the costs of feeding the flock can really add up.

A sit-down lunch may be too long for a networking meeting, particularly if you're in a restaurant where the dining experience is an hour and a half. Once the networking agenda has been completed (see Chapter 5), time will start to hang heavy with a contact you hadn't known before and with whom you can't share residual gossip ("So how're Marge and the kids?") over dessert and coffee. Finally, bear in mind that the bodily requirements of chewing and swallowing can get in the way of graceful give-'n'-take networking. You'll talk—leaving your poached salmon untouched—as the contact munches self-consciously through his broccoli surprise. Eventually, he may conclude it's his turn to talk a while, at which time you must plow through your chow at warp speed in order to catch up.

If you decide to network over lunch, find eating places that serve small portions, and select food that doesn't drool on you when you eat fast (grilled chicken breast is fairly safe and splatter-free). Look for "interesting" places to eat, meaning inexpensive.

Because the networking meeting is a favor to you, agree to meet at the contact's convenience. "Power breakfasts" are coming on strong as an extension of the number of hours in a business day. A breakfast of half a grapefruit, a toasted English muffin and black coffee at 7:00 A.M. may be your contact's idea of a good get-together. If you're not an early riser, this regimen can really fry your biorhythms. It's more common for businesspeople to go Dutch for breakfast than for lunch, but still be ready to reach for the check.

"Asking Around" in the Association

In our discussion about developing your list of potential networking contacts, we paid a lot of attention to professional associations, community groups, fraternal organizations and the like. They're fruitful fields for the serious networker, but watch out when you till those fields: land mines may be hidden in their rich soil.

Most associations and professional groups are, at heart, designed to foster formal and informal exchange of information; they are, in large measure, networking organizations. However, the collective good and professional interests of the entire membership are supposed to get top priority; your personal job search or career development agenda shouldn't overshadow the collective purposes and activities of the association.

Some of the most savage attacks on networking are coming—quite justifiably—from sincere members of organizations who are tired of seeing job seekers plunk down the membership fee, grab the membership list and then use the organization as nothing more than a private networking playground. The strength and viability of these organizations depend on the willingness of members to contribute, not just take. People who join such a group simply to further their own interests are seen as hypocritical, self-serving and manipulative. Do it, and you'll earn a bad reputation for yourself and for networking.

You need not exclude such a group from your networking efforts if you are an active member, attend its conferences and draw on its resources while participating

---

FOR YOUR INFORMATION

WHERE TO FIND ASSOCIATIONS

The definitive source is *Encyclopedia of Associations,* published annually by Gale Research. The three-volume set lists some 25,000 trade and professional groups, ranging from absinthe connoisseurs to zoo protection activists. Listings include name, address, phone number, size, officers, and a description of each group's structure and purpose. You can order the encyclopedia from Gale (Box 33477, Detroit, MI 48232-5477), but why not use it free at the reference desk in any public library?

Be wary of databases and direct-mail lists that claim to be "proprietary lists" or to have access to "the hidden job market." Many of them contain stale information or are reissues of other databases. Ask to see their product, and be clear on how their costs are computed.

actively in its agenda. Becoming a regular contributor and visible figure is a terrific way of marketing your skills and abilities. Volunteering your time may seem wasteful when you face the more fundamental priority of finding work, but remember a most fundamental networking axiom: "What goes around comes around." The more you go around, the more chances you'll have for opportunities to come around.

If you honestly don't have enough time to participate in the affairs of a group you're thinking of joining, don't join. If your main purpose is to glom on to the membership roster, try to get it another way. Borrow a friend's copy, then try cold-call networking into the membership without using the subterfuge of feigned affiliation.

Get the Ball Rolling

Enough preamble; it's time to do something. Take a deep breath. Select the name of a friend or colleague from your Proximity contact list and pick up the phone. Use this as a model for your part of the conversation:

> Beth? This is Leon. I was hoping I might be able to prevail on you for a little help. I don't know if you've heard that MinorTech has been bought by Acquire-All, but we all think our jobs are in serious danger, and I want to begin to test the waters. I haven't had to run a job search in 15 years, Beth, and the thought of hitting the job market is, well, a little unsettling. [pause slightly]
>
> I was wondering if I could sit down with you for 45 minutes or an hour, for a "networking"-type meeting. I promise you, I'm not going to hit on you or your company for a job, and I don't expect that you will magically know of available openings out there. I really would welcome the chance to pick your brain about what's happening in the artificial intelligence industry. At this point in my search, it would be very helpful to me to be able to sit down with someone I know and am comfortable with and get some practice describing my background, what I have to offer and why I'm in the job market. [pause slightly]
>
> I'd be happy to meet with you any time, at your convenience, but since what I'm trying to show off here is my game face, it would be best if we could arrange to sit down at your office rather than in a social setting.

If your request strikes the proper balance between being low-key and being directive, chances are you'll get the networking meeting on your terms. With this script, you've subtly changed the stakes by letting the contact know that your request for help is slightly more structured and formal than your prior relationship would normally suggest.

Other opening phrases can carry the same signal that a friend or acquaintance should listen with a more attentive ear:

Bill, for once I'm not calling to borrow your lawnmower. I wonder if I could prevail on you for a different kind of favor?

Or:

Janice, this may sound a little stilted, but I was hoping I could call on your friendship in a way I never have before.

These openers may sound a little heavy, but they'll ensure that your request is chewed slowly and not swallowed too fast.

FOR YOUR INFORMATION

FAMOUS WORDS ABOUT FRIENDSHIP

☆   I get by with a little help from my friends.—John Lennon and Paul McCartney.

☆   We all praise fidelity, but the true friend pays the penalty when he supports those whom Fortune crushes.—Lucan (60 A.D.).

☆   Among the other evils which being unarmed brings you, it causes you to be despised.—Machiavelli, *The Prince*.

☆   But in deed/A friend is never known till a man have need.—John Heywood (1579).

☆   The best mirror is an old friend.—George Herbert (1630).

Upping the Ante

Sooner or later, you're going to ask for a networking meeting with someone you don't know. The lubrication of friendship and proximity will be absent. You may no longer use the ice-breaker: "I just want to practice to see if I can present a clear product profile." About this time, many job seekers develop a strong approach–avoidance conflict and a simultaneous sudden interest in daytime TV.

This is the time to suck it up and go for it. When you do, and you find out how easy it is and how friendly most people are, you're going to wonder why you were so apprehensive. You'll pick up a pail you thought was full of water, only to discover it's empty. Your energy will rise dramatically. Rank cheerleading? No; an objective description of what scores of successful networkers have reported: Once you're in, the water's fine.

Call or Write?

A lively debate continues among networkers about whether the best approach is to phone or to write. Both techniques have their virtues. Judge what works best for you according to what makes you most comfortable or what is called for by the specific information you have about your contact.

The beauty of calling is that if you can succeed in getting the Perspective contact or Power contact on the line, it's harder for him to ignore or deflect the request for help. An immediate response is called for, and the one most frequently given is "Yes." The trick is to reach the contact without being screened out, put on indefinite hold or shunted to the human resources department by a well-trained secretary who protects the boss from low-priority intrusions.

A letter will usually get through and be read. A good introductory note can set up the stage for a follow-up phone call, without the pressure of having to "cut to the chase" in the first few seconds ("Hi, you don't know me but . . ."). It can mention the name of the person who referred you, state why you want the networking meeting and what the contact is supposed to know, provide a brief thumbnail sketch of your background and objectives, and, if you like, serve as a low-pressure delivery vehicle for your resume (which otherwise is considered a high-pressure sales brochure).

For the many networkers who hate cold calling or who consider a telephone call a form of surprise attack, a letter can seem like a calmer, quieter approach. Indeed, in an age when telemarketing is on the upswing and bombards us with unsolicited calls and requests, a letter may be the best way not to get lumped in with the hucksters selling time-share condos in the Everglades.

The problems with a letter are:

1. It too may be screened, particularly if it includes a resume. Many secretaries are instructed that any letter containing a resume is to be forwarded to Human Resources or deposited in the Round File.

2. Even if it's read, there's no pressure for an immediate response.

When deciding between a phone call or a letter, ask yourself five basic questions:

1. How comfortable, succinct and articulate can I be on the phone, particularly with people I don't know?

2. How great a disparity in age, power or status is there between me and the contact I want to network with? (The greater the disparity, the more appropriate a letter.)

3. What form of communication is the contact likely to get more of—letters or phone calls? (Choose whichever he gets less of; don't throw yourself in with all the other lemmings.)

4. Does my situation require a lot of explaining or involve a complicated chronological sequence of prior events or contacts? (If so, a letter is better.)

5. How's my writing ability? Can I compose a direct, candid, well-organized letter without tripping over grammar and syntax or launching into something that sounds like a presidential inaugural address?

If you're trying to cold-call a contact without the benefit of a friend or colleague as a referral, a letter may be a better choice. People tend to erect a set of defenses when a voice on the phone says, "Hi, you don't know me but . . . ." In such situations, a letter may seem more respectful, more measured and less presumptuous.

When you're working off the launch pad of Proximity referrals, using the phone will allow you to cover more ground in less time with fewer stamps, and you should try phoning a few networking leads. You might call between 8:30 and 9:00 A.M. or after 5:00 P.M.—the times when many people are more likely to pick up their own phones. Monday mornings aren't great (the contact will be trying to wade through the task of setting up the coming week) and late Friday afternoon is irritating.

Use the do-unto-others Golden Rule when networking: Don't call anyone at a time when you would dislike being called.

Surviving the Screen

Be prepared to have your call answered by an experienced, professional secretary whose job requires him or her to be interposed between you and your desired contact. The phone dialogue might go something like this (editorial comments are in parentheses):

Secretary (Sec)*:* Mr. Wellington's office.

Networker (NW)*:* Hi. Richard Wright calling. Is he in, please?

Sec: May I ask what this is in reference to? (The screen is drawn.)

NW: His friend, Fred Ott, strongly suggested I call. I was hoping to ask Mr. Wellington a quick question. (The secretary is now at risk. She doesn't want to offend Ott, yet she can't simply abandon her role as screener. She buys time.)

Sec: I'm sorry, he's away from his desk right now. May I have him call you back? (She's hitting you with a counter ploy. Don't lose control; stay with an unfailingly cooperative tone.)

NW: That would be fine. My number is . . . you know, I'm going to be in and out of meetings all afternoon, and I'd hate to catch him up in a game of phone tag. Besides (mock-confession), I'm not even sure he'd recognize my name. It probably makes more sense for me to try to call him back. Is there a time later this afternoon when I might be able to reach him for a quick call?

Sec: His calender looks awfully busy for the rest of the afternoon, Mr. Wright. I'm sorry. (She's not going to roll over and play dead before she's had a chance to confer with her boss.)

NW: (reminding her of the contact and reheating the risk to her, but continuing to try to make the pressure sound helpful): Yes, Fred told me Mr. Wellington's a really busy man, and I don't want to make a pest of myself, but I was hoping to hook up with him in the next day or so. Tell me, is there a time tomorrow morning when it would be convenient for me to try to call?

Sec: Well, he has an 8:30 meeting that I expect to run until about 10:00, then an 11:00 meeting downtown.

NW: If I try to reach him at about 10:15, would that make sense?

Sec: Well, yes, you could try that. (It's a draw. She has surrendered the screen, but she has won herself time to talk to Wellington to see how to treat you tomorrow. In your favor, there is a definite next step at a definite time. That's good.)

NW: (upbeat, pleasant): Fine. I'll call then. I appreciate your help. Oh, may I ask your name?

Sec: (She will pause here as she decides what to do. She knows that you're trying to outflank her official role as an impassive screen and turn her into a human being, but she has no right or reason to withhold her identity. By using a reserved, formal tone, however, she may inform you that she's on to your ploy to humanize her.) My name is Mrs. Carmody.

NW: (The best time to address her by name is when you call tomorrow. For now, just reiterate that you appreciate her efforts on your behalf.) Thanks again for your help. I'll call tomorrow at about 10:15.

The following morning, **at the appointed time**:

NW: Good morning, Mrs. Carmody. It's Richard Wright again. How are we doing for getting through to Mr. Wellington? (Because she told you to call, she's now on your side of the desk, supposedly helping you through the screen to her boss.)

If she then tells you that Wellington is in fact unavailable and really will have to call you back, you have no choice but to go into the passive mode, leave your phone number, and hope that his sense of obligation to his friend Fred Ott will carry the day. If you don't hear from Wellington within several days, you can try one more call to Mrs. Carmody and diplomatically try to regain some control:

NW: Mrs. Carmody, this is Richard Wright. I haven't yet heard from Mr. Wellington. I really don't want to be a nuisance, but as I mentioned when you and I spoke, I was hoping to catch him sometime this week. What's our best step at this point?

FOR YOUR INFORMATION

THE VELVET HAMMERLOCK: HOW TO LEAN ON PEOPLE

In the course of networking, many people will make promises about how they'll help you, but, without being tactless or pushy, how do you ensure that the offered help is delivered?

Two principles govern successful, diplomatic pressure:

1. Ask how the person wants to be leaned on.
2. Couch the pressure as if it's for the other person's convenience or benefit.

Rather than telling the person that you will check up to make sure he delivers, clarify that there will be a next step by asking what that step should be: "How about if I check back with you in a couple of days to see where things stand?"

Any time you're tempted to say, "I'm going to . . . ," substitute something collaborative: "How about if we . . . ?" or "What's our next step?" or "Would it make sense if we . . . ?" If you really want to be direct, try the "triple-A technique" ("*A*sk for *A*lternatives *A*ccommodatingly"). This approach forces a choice between alternatives: "Would it be better if I follow up with the commission directly, or would you prefer that I touch base with you first?"

The KISS Principle: Keep it simple, stupid

When you're past Mrs. Carmody and your prospective contact is on the phone, it's time to throw your pitch. Let's freeze-frame your delivery for an instructive run-through.

The Ice-Breaker

You are identifying yourself and your referral source, explaining the purpose of the call, and (very important!) qualifying the contact—that is, telling him why he's of potential value and what he's supposed to know:

> Mr. Wellington, Fred Ott suggested I call to see if I might get a little informal advice and counsel from you. Fred tells me you have real expertise in multi-level marketing and have spent a lot of time both investigating who the players are in that industry and developing your own organization.
>
> I recently resigned as Regional Sales Manager for DataSpecific after they carved up my territories into a crazy-quilt. I've decided, at age 46, that it's time to think about looking into new and more autonomous approaches to sales and marketing. Fred said your experience and perspective might help save me a lot of wasted time and energy.
>
> What I was hoping we might do is sit down for a few minutes, at your convenience, and chat about multilevel marketing. I'm curious to know where the industry is going and who the reputable organizations are. I'd also welcome any feedback you could offer about how well my background and skills would translate into the multilevel marketing field.

The "Decompression"

This is one of the most important steps in the process, yet many networkers do it awkwardly or not at all. You must give a sincere reassurance that your request is low-stakes and time-limited. Because so many black-hearted networkers are guilty of false and deceptive decompression, you may want to consider a "double decompression":

> Let me emphasize that my purpose in asking to meet with you isn't to hit you up for a job. I know that a lot of people are asking for these "networking" meetings to get in the door, then they go into a full-court press and ask for employment. I promise I won't do that to you—and I wouldn't embarrass Fred Ott by acting inappropriately toward someone he was good enough to refer me to. At this point in my job search, I'm trying to gather information and get a clear image of the marketplace. If you know of any specific opportunities, of course

I'd be interested. But I'm not calling with the expectation that you have or know of any openings or opportunities.

Scheduling

We noted earlier that face-to-face meetings are best—if you can get them without being overly aggressive. When you are exerting subtle pressure, the key is to ask about the person's preferences and cast your suggestions in terms of the convenience of the contact:

> I was hoping we might get together for a short meeting. I see no reason why it would have to go longer than 45 minutes. As for scheduling, it would be completely at your convenience. I could drop in on you at your office if that's best, meet you some place after work or perhaps hook up for breakfast. What would work best for you?

If the contact describes himself as "really jammed up right now" and suggests that May 15, 1997, would be a good time to meet, you can both defer and counterpress by putting a gentle time-frame around your request:

> If that's the first time we could get together, so be it. But because there is a multilevel marketing conference in St. Louis in three weeks, I was hoping we might squeeze in a quick meeting before then, so I can go in better prepared to evaluate what I hear there. I don't want to make a pest of myself, but I would be grateful if I could grab a short stretch of your time before the 23rd.

If a timely face-to-face meeting isn't possible, your first fallback position is to ask whether the contact will network on the phone. Don't assume that because the person is on the phone with you, now is the time to launch into your two-minute drill. Again, ask the contact's preferences:

> Fred told me how busy your schedule is, and I can certainly understand if it isn't possible to meet personally. It would still be very helpful to me if I could have a couple of minutes of your time on the phone. Have you time to talk now, or would another time be more convenient for me to call you back?

Mrs. Carmody 1, Networker 0

The Mrs. Carmodys of the business world will often succeed in screening you away from their bosses. Instead of agreeing to a set time for you to call back, they will insist: "I'll have Mr. Wellington return your call" or (worse) "I'll give Mr.

Wellington your number." If you don't hear back from Mr. Wellington in a couple of days, you can try a follow-up call or two, but don't keep hammering with call after call. Overpersistance can be a major turn-off. If you don't hear back from Wellington, try a brief letter that explains who you are and what you want.

A Networking "Chase Letter"

Dear Mr. Wellington:

I'm sorry we've been unable to hook up by phone; let me explain who I am and why I was calling. In a recent conversation with Fred Ott, I mentioned that, having resigned from my position as Regional Sales Manager at DataSpecific, I am exploring the multilevel marketing industry. Fred immediately thought of you and mentioned that you had researched the industry carefully before starting your business and are a font of knowledge about trends, pluses, minuses and industry leaders in multilevel marketing.

I was calling to see whether we might arrange, at your convenience, a brief "networking" meeting in which I might get your views about the industry and the best approach for someone like me to research a career shift into multilevel marketing.

Let me emphasize as strongly as I can that my purpose isn't to request employment with your organization, nor do I expect that you know of any particular jobs or openings at this point. Fred suggested that, in just an hour of your time, I could learn a lot that would help me target and focus my efforts, get a little exposure, and perhaps come away with some suggestions about other people I would do well to meet.

I will follow up shortly by phone to see if we might schedule a time to meet. If it's more convenient for you to give Mrs. Carmody some possible meeting times, I'll be pleased to schedule with her and not trouble you further. I very much appreciate your help.

Sincerely,

Richard Wright

If these approaches don't work, you might try calling Fred Ott back and mentioning that you're having a tough time getting Wellington to respond. Fred may choose to use up some of his valuable currency by leaning on Wellington, but you should understand that the renewed pressure may make Wellington a little testy, even if he does eventually agree to see you. If he's a valuable contact, it may be worth the extra effort, risk and obligation. (If Fred agrees to follow up personally, you really owe him a few favors.) If all this deft, tactful pressure doesn't pay off, put a big, black line through Wellington's name on your networking list.

Conferences, Conventions and Meetings

Gatherings of professional associations, fraternal organizations and community groups are veritable hotbeds of networking leads. Attend as many as you can, grab any and all attendance lists, collect as many business cards as possible and try to make a sincere contribution. In other words, your networking efforts at such gatherings shouldn't look like networking efforts, unless the sole purpose of the organization is to provide an opportunity to develop networking contacts.

One of the fastest ways to earn yourself a bad rap as a self-serving weasel is to try to work through a network meeting agenda (see Chapter 5) with individuals whom you collar at a conference. Everyone attending a conference is out to maximize his exposure, and if you pin someone in a corner behind the relish tray and monopolize his lunch hour or break time, you'll make an enemy. Instead, exchange a few words of introduction, then ask for leave to follow up after the conference:

> Mr. Wellington? Hi, I'm Richard Wright. I don't believe we've met, but Fred Ott has lots of nice things to say about your knowledge of multilevel marketing. I've recently resigned from my position as Regional Sales Manager with DataSpecific, and I'm taking a hard look at multilevel marketing. Look, I don't want to pull you away from the conference and colleagues now, but would it be OK if I called on you after the conference? I really would be grateful if we might arrange an informal "networking" meeting.

Face-to-face, in public, Wellington is far more likely to say, "Yeah, sure, gimme a call" than to blow you off. He'll then probably forget all about meeting you, but you won't. After the conference, you can proceed with what we'll call "Wright's Revenge":

Mrs. Carmody: Mr. Wellington's office.

You: Hi, this is Richard Wright calling. When I was chatting with Mr. Wellington at the conference the other day, he said to give him a call to schedule an appointment. Do you have his calendar handy? (Touché.)

Requests by Letter

If you decide you'd be more comfortable making your overture by letter, the tone and length suggested in the earlier follow-up letter to Wellington—minus the reference to the attempt to get through by phone—are appropriate. The letter shouldn't be longer than about two-thirds of a page; write more and you confront the reader with a daunting challenge in just wading through it.

There's a common tendency to *overwrite* networking letters—to include too much irrelevant personal detail and try to use the letter to work through issues that are proper topics for the meeting itself. About as many letters are too breezy and presumptuous as are too formal. Strive for a direct, conversational tone. Use strong topic sentences and active verbs—everything your English teacher drummed into you in the seventh grade.

"Cold-Call" Request Letter

Dear Ms. Schmidt:

I have recently returned to the Chicago area (I was raised in Winnetka and did my undergraduate work in economics at Northwestern) from San Francisco, where for the past four years I was director of development for the Bay-to-Bay Players, a repertory company and artists' consortium with a $4 million annual budget.

When I mentioned to a few local acquaintances in Chicago that I want to move from nonprofit development into private-sector entrepreneurial marketing, several promptly mentioned you. It seems that as head of the Women's Entrepreneurial Forum, you are well-known and highly respected in the local entrepreneurial, venture capital and investment banking communities.

I'm writing in the hope that we might get together for some informal networking. Without intending to enlist you as a career counselor, I would welcome any thoughts you might have about how to attack this transition: is it a matter of going back to school, repackaging myself or making some interim move? Because my local network is limited, I also would be most grateful to learn of other entrepreneurs to whom I might introduce myself. I've enclosed a copy of my resume, just to give you a better feel for my background.

Let me plan on following up with you in a few days to see if we might arrange an introductory meeting. Thanks very much.

Sincerely,

Deidre Hubell

Above and beyond the straightforward approach in Deidre's letter, note how she "framed" the inclusion of her resume. Remember: a resume is a sales brochure, a request for employment. Including the resume in your letter may suggest that you're looking for an interview, not a networking meeting. While decompressing her request for some networking, Deidre also decompressed the presence of her resume.

Getting contacts to warm up enough to spend some time with you isn't a matter of uttering ritual phrases or magic words. It's a matter of human nature. If you're pleasant, candid and sensitive to the other person's time and priorities, you'll get most of the meetings you want—however and wherever requested. Then the real fun begins.

"It happens . . . just take a few moments, relax, collect your thoughts and I'm sure your name will come to you."

5

What Goes On in a Networking Meeting

The vast majority of your networking interactions will have no form, structure, or agenda. They will happen on street corners, in between motions at the board meeting, at the end of long business telephone calls, and on the commuter train home.

These snatches of gossip are not generally dignified by calling them "networking interactions," and you won't ask yourself who has a responsibility to make sure they maintain a sense of purpose and direction. But every time you come away from one of these chance exchanges, you'll be a little better informed, a little wiser than before. You won't sweat this lack of structure and you won't worry yourself with whether the exchange went well or poorly; you'll just file the new data away for future use.

However, the moment an informal street-corner swap of information escalates into a scheduled "networking meeting," your palms begin to sweat. Performance anxiety and fear of ridicule set in. "I'm going to be judged," you think. "I've got to be good. I've got to be on. If I blow this, I'll really humiliate myself and damage my prospects in the job market."

Your anxiety is understandable but overblown. First, if you're at all prepared and pleasant, it's pretty hard to utterly punt a networking meeting. Second, you should understand from the outset that a certain percentage of meetings are going to be lemons. On occasion, you and the contact simply will fail to connect; the meeting will be short, forced and stilted. Some contacts may display hostility, frustration at not being able to help more, stupidity, and, perhaps, some really terrible judgment. It all goes with the territory. But most of your meetings will be comfortable and at least somewhat informative, and some will be exhilarating.

The more good meetings you have, the less the occasional bomb will hit you. Remember that networking is a numbers game. Play early, play often, and let the numbers take care of themselves.

Who Drives the Meeting?

The best networking meetings are those with the least apparent structure, the least amount of posturing or subtle jockeying for leverage, the most casual and comfortable flow of ideas and the most spontaneity. Both parties go with the flow—or so it appears. A relaxed networking meeting starts with an appropriate request for help and moves into a convincing decompression. The contact has a clear idea of what he's being consulted about, and the networker is well prepared. Once the meeting is under way, that comfortable tone can be maintained if the networker constantly checks the pulse of the proceedings and has mastered some techniques for keeping the tone light and the pace brisk.

War Story: Turned into a pillar of salt

Some years ago, a midlevel member of the White House staff—an affable and outgoing sort—lost his job in a move meant to save face for his superior. His "reward" for falling quietly on his sword was an assurance that some fairly awesome networking referrals would come his way and "people would be eager to help." His first meeting, scheduled at arm's length through respective secretaries, was with a former member of the Cabinet who was the wife of a powerful senator and who remained a powerful woman in her own right. She had an established reputation for eating weaklings for lunch.

The networker was ushered into an empty office by a secretary who gestured toward a comfortable-looking chair. When he sat down, most of his six-and-a-half-foot frame disappeared into the unusually soft seat cushions, and he found himself looking up at the world across the tops of his knees, now folded inches from his face. He then noted that the desk of his contact sat atop a three-inch raised platform.

The door opened and in swept a tall, energetic woman wearing a broad, intense smile. She sat down so rapidly he had no time to rise. She stretched the smile still more broadly across her powerful features, cocked her head and said nothing. So thoroughly "unempowered" was the networker by this time that all he could do was smile mutely back at her. Fully ten interminable seconds crawled by until she finally said, in a quiet, clipped voice, "Talk to me, you son-of-a-bitch. You called this meeting." The networker has little recollection of the rest of this meeting.

FOR YOUR INFORMATION

GROUND RULES FOR A NETWORKING MEETING

1. A networking meeting must have direction.
2. The networker is responsible for setting the direction of the meeting and keeping things moving.
3. Most problems in networking meetings arise from confusion about the process, not the content.
4. If things seem to be going wrong or going nowhere, the networker must take the blame and clarify the agenda before diving back into content. For example:

> Bill, I realize from your last question that I didn't explain clearly that I moved from civil engineering into construction project management before my years in Australia. Let me review my career chronology. Then I'd welcome your thoughts on how to reestablish myself in project management or construction litigation support back here in the States.

A networking meeting isn't an interview. Unlike an interview, responsibility for the direction and pace of a networking meeting rests with the networker, not with the contact. The networker owns the meeting, sets the agenda, and takes the blame if he handles his role poorly.

The Play's the Thing

A good networking meeting is a play in six acts, usually unfolding in a logical and predictable sequence:

Act 1. Setting the Stage (clarifying the agenda, allocating responsibilities).

Act 2. Frame of Reference (providing the contact with information).

Act 3. What to Say in Q&A (exchanging information, educating, learning and refining the focus).

Act 4. The Name Game (extending the network and obtaining more contacts).

Act 5. Closing Up and Getting Out.

Act 6. The Follow-Up (closing the loop and delivering on the deal).

This chapter looks at each act in detail.

Act 1. Setting the Stage

How much time you spend on introductory pleasantries and setting the stage will depend on how thoroughly the purpose of the meeting and the roles of the players were discussed when you requested the meeting. A lot of meetings get off to a confused, mushy start because the contact doesn't know (or has forgotten):

☆   Who referred the networker and why; what the contact is supposed to know that will be of use to the networker.

☆   The networker's status and time frame: Is the networker thinking of making a change? Currently employed and running a confidential job search? Unemployed and working full-time on job search efforts? Just finishing school? Planning on making a change next year?

☆   What the networker expects to get out of the meeting.

In every meeting, concentrate first on the process by taking a moment to reset the stage. One of the best ways to discipline yourself is to imagine that the contact has just said, "Hi. How can I help you?" Respond to this question and everyone will be on firm footing at the start. Here is an example:

Marlene, I want to thank you again for taking the time to see me on such short notice. I know how busy you are, so I very much appreciate your help, and I promise I'll keep this short and sweet. You may remember that when we talked last week, I mentioned that for the past three years I've been the chief legislative aide for state senator John LaRousse and that he had just lost in the primary. His whole staff will be out of work at the end of the year. I want to get a head start on developing new employment now, and if I can develop something attractive, John understands that I'll resign immediately to take it.

As I'll flesh out in a minute, it was only in my last job that I moved into legislative and government work. But I'm already finding that most people assume I want to stay in politics, when actually I'd like to get back toward my old career path in developing and managing human service programs. Several people I've networked with, particularly Stan Wolfe, thought of you immediately and said that as a strategic planning consultant to foundations and nonprofits, you were familiar with a lot of organizations and knew key people in that sector. I hope I made it clear when we spoke that my purpose in calling wasn't to request a job with your consulting firm. I know a lot of people turn these "networking" meetings into pleas for a job, but I assure you that's not my objective.

It would be helpful, however, if I could summarize my background and current priorities—both to get some visibility and see if they make sense to you—and perhaps pick your brain about trends you see, areas I might explore, or other contacts I should try to meet with.

There are several points to observe as you set the stage. Your opening monologue has to sound like human conversation and not like a rehearsed, perfunctory recitation. All spark or warmth will leave the meeting if there's a nearly audible *click!* as you switch on your "canned" announcement and drone through

---

FOR YOUR INFORMATION

THE $100,000 SOCCER GAME

To remind networkers to be aware of each contact's level of sophistication, a career counselor insisted that each workshop participant "describe clearly what you are and what you do as if I were a seven-year-old." Several years later, the counselor got a call from one of the participants. "I've got a great anecdote if you ever use the seven-year-old exercise again," the man said. "Ever since your seminar, I've made sure that my kids can describe what I do very clearly, which isn't easy because I'm in environmental toxic waste remediation consulting.

"Before a recent soccer game, my ten-year-old was talking with friends about whose dad did what. During the game's second half, one of the fathers approached me and said, 'I understand your firm does toxic waste remediation?' I just closed on a $100,000 contract with him. My child had explained to another child enough about what I do so that he could describe it to his father. You were right: frame of reference is everything."

some ritual disclaimers. Career changers who are networking with contacts in other fields should take a moment to gauge the contact's level of sophistication and understanding about any technical content, jargon, or shoptalk that may come out. If you begin using terms or constructs your contact doesn't understand, he won't stop you to ask for explanation more than once or twice. To do so would betray ignorance, and human nature doesn't like to do that repeatedly. Instead, the contact will hide behind a vacant grin and nod his head mechanically as your words whoosh in one ear and out the other.

Act 2. Frame of Reference

Once the stage is set and you're sure that you and the contact are working on the same plot, you shift from structuring the setting to providing the contact with a Frame of Reference (F.O.R.) about you.

> Lloyd, maybe the best way to start is for me to take just a second to give you a quick thumbnail sketch of my background—what I've been doing and what I want to do next.

Then you proceed with your two-minute drill.

This approach sounds easy, but it's at this point that many networking meetings jump the rails and never get back on track again. The purpose of the F.O.R. is to deliver a brief, concise summary so the contact has enough information to ask relevant questions. It isn't intended to provide a sales pitch, an encyclopedic history of your life, or answers to questions that haven't been asked yet.

A frame encloses a subject and sets boundaries. If you're still giving a "brief summary" after ten minutes, you're depriving the contact of the chance to talk, to ask questions, and to be the wise expert. The contact may unwittingly abet your verbosity by asking, during your two-minute drill, questions that invite you to elaborate on some point, then another question about your elaboration, and so on. If that happens, gracefully field and hold the question until you've finished framing your personal profile:

> That's a good question, Judy, and one of the things I want to discuss with you. Before I explain more about that, let me just take a second to finish my thumbnail sketch and make sure you have a broad overview of where I'm coming from and where I think I want to go.

At this stage of any networking meeting, you should ask yourself, "If this meeting ended right now, could this contact describe me accurately to someone else in terms of level, role or function and setting?" That's the most elementary requirement of any successful networking meeting, and you should work hard to maintain gentle discipline to achieve it. There will be plenty of time to meander and elaborate after you've constructed your frame.

Act 3. What to Say in Q&A

In Chapter 1, we stated that networking has three fundamental goals: (1) to compile information, (2) to gain maximum exposure and (3) to gather names in order to continue to expand your network. By this point in the meeting, the exposure goal has been met (at least minimally): You showed up, you've been seen, and you've made a (presumably) positive impression and provided a bare-bones frame of reference. Even if the meeting produces no further benefit beyond this exposure, it has been worth your time.

In the give and take of information, the meeting can really get interesting. What's of interest to any particular networker depends on his needs and on where he stands in the whole job search or career transition process.

Networkers' Conventional Job Search

Job seekers who are lucky enough to have a linear career path and a clear market identity ("I am a senior processing engineer manager in pharmaceuticals") need less emphasis on defining and focusing the product than on finding out where the jobs are. Mostly, they seek market information, and they should ask the contact questions that cut to the chase.

Networking Guidesheet for Conventional Job Seekers

The Product

☆ Is my frame of reference clear to you? Does my prior career path make sense?

☆ In light of my F.O.R., is my job search objective clear? Is it realistic? Have I articulated my areas of technical skills (TSs) clearly? Have I provided clear and convincing examples of my experience and transferable abilities (TAs)?

☆ What new skills or technical credentials, if any, do you think I need to be an attractive candidate for the kind and level of position I want?

☆ Is there anything about my prior employment history or present circumstances that you think might create problems or issues for potential employers?

☆ What skills, abilities, and personal qualities do you think are most desirable in high-performing people at my level in my field?

☆ How did you get into this field? Is there anything about your career path or progression that you think is relevant to my thinking or my job search efforts?

☆ Are there other industries, sectors, or roles to which you think my skills and abilities would transfer readily? Do you think I should research or explore other directions?

The General Market

☆ What general economic, operational, and employment trends do you see in the industry? Who are the industry leaders? Why?

☆ What sort or size of company do you think would be most interested in skills and experience like mine? Why?

☆ What's a realistic compensation range for someone with my skills and abilities? What benefits and other perks can I expect?

☆ How would you characterize the prospects for advancement for someone like me right now? What factors do you think most affect growth and advancement?

☆ Do you think my prospects would be better with a (bigger vs. smaller; mature vs. rapid-growth/entrepreneurial; start-up vs. established; centralized vs. diversified; single-site vs. multisite; flat vs. hierarchical; public vs. closely held; vertically integrated vs. horizontally integrated) company? Why do you think so?

☆ What do you see as the long-term trends or prospects in my field?

☆ What are the best sources (directories, periodicals, databases, associations, texts, etc.) to find out more about what's going on in this area? Do you know of anyone who has a broad perspective of my field? Would it make sense for me to talk with that person?

Targeting Specific Leads

☆ Are you personally familiar with any companies in this area, or with individuals in any of those companies?

☆ Do you know of any openings or specific opportunities for someone like me right now?

☆ Have you heard of any events or developments that suggest a particular company might have a need for someone like me?

☆ What have you heard about the company (in terms of reputation, market share, profitability, hiring trends, management style or "culture," job security, strategic plans, effect of external factors or conditions)?

☆ Where's the best place to look for news of jobs or openings?

This guidesheet is intended to highlight areas of discussion and inquiry, not to be a punch-list for aggressive direct examination of the "witness." A pleasant and effective networking meeting involves discussion and elaboration, not a barrage of questions from the networker. Expect, for example, to spend some time (after the two-minute drill) amplifying and highlighting your skills and experience. Be ready with specific examples to illustrate your past accomplishments. Above all, don't be so persistent in your questioning that you leave the contact no time or opportunity to ask questions.

A meeting that should be built on give-and-take assumes too often the confrontational structure of a screening interview: "I'll pitch and you hit and then you can pitch and I'll hit." That level of control and structure is counterproductive to building rapport. Try to keep things loose.

Career Changers' Agenda: A whole different game

Many people who are shifting career roles or moving into new settings these days report an unsettling lack of focus. Here is a typical complaint:

> I can describe what I was, but I won't know what I am until I'm in my next job. There are probably a lot of things I could do, but I don't even know what some of them are. How do I describe my objectives without either arbitrarily ruling out a lot of potential opportunities or being so broad that I appear to have no direction at all?

If you're a career shifter, the bad news is that there's no simple way to inventory all the roles and settings that might be a good fit for you; the playing field of human endeavor is simply too great. You could read through the Department of Labor's *Directory of Occupational Titles* (the DOT), but be aware that it lists only those jobs that the government has seen fit to reduce to a terse description and a Standard Industrial Code (SIC). It's dull reading, but might be worth an hour or two of your time, if only to jump-start your thought processes.

The best ways to get a handle on what you might want to do in a career shift are: (1) talk to other people about what they do and (2) present them with a "menu" of your skills, abilities, interests, aptitudes, and temperament and ask them to brainstorm with you. You won't be expected or required to have a clear focus, particularly at the outset of your career transition efforts, or to have all the answers. (Getting those answers is what networking is for.) You will be expected to have engaged in some structured self-assessment.

As the networking process goes on and you meet a variety of people, learn what they do, and "try on" their work and life-style, either you'll find your interest whetted or you'll discover that what sounded like a neat way to earn a living isn't for you. For career shifters, much of networking amounts to what doctors call a "rule-out diagnosis": by exploring and discarding as many potential options as you can, you dramatically narrow the array of viable options. Early-stage networking for career shifters is a 20-questions game with the world of work: you try to cut the playing field down to more manageable proportions by eliminating as many types of roles and settings as you can. This initial activity produces a greater sense of focus and an ability to provide an increasingly precise description of the type of role or setting that would best suit you. For a lot of networkers— particularly gregarious extroverts—this process of sampling other people's work lives can be fascinating.

FOR YOUR INFORMATION

CANVASS THE UNIVERSE WHEN CHANGING CAREERS

Julie holds a PhD in American folklore, has displayed her sculpture in juried art shows, and is an expert on urban graffiti as an art form. She was dean of students at a prestigious art school but became frustrated with administrative tasks and academic bureaucracy. When told that it was time to part ways, she decided to use her year's severance "to explore what's out there."

The diversity of Julie's contacts was staggering. Over the next few months, she learned about zoo administration. She checked out a foundation that was considering sending artists to paint the Amazon rainforest. The director of a renowned arboretum took a liking to her. A women's rights group found her accomplishments impressive. Julie found this career sampling invigorating—for about six months, until her need to be productive resurfaced. Despite all her contacts, she still felt unfocused.

Julie continued to network widely and finally found a fit. She now coordinates extension programs for a major university, including curriculum design, marketing, program evaluation and new-program development.

Networking meetings that involve career changers often loosen up quickly and become comfortable for both parties. The contact isn't expected to be a great expert on some industry; he's asked to talk about himself and his own experience, which most people enjoy doing.

Networking Guidesheet for Career Changers

Tell Me about You

☆   How did you get into this field?

☆   What made you decide that this was the kind of career for you to pursue?

☆   What training, special credentials, or experience were prerequisite to getting hired in your field or your position?

☆   What are your responsibilities and what do you actually do during a representative day of work?

☆   What functions or activities are included in your work? What are the greatest satisfactions you derive from this kind of work?

☆   What don't you like about this field or about your job?

☆   What's the typical career progression in this field? If there isn't one, where do you see your career going?

☆   What other career options will your present role allow? If you continue doing what you're doing now, what kinds of options will be precluded in the future?

☆   To what extent are gender, age, race or other factors relevant to advancement in this field?

Tell Me about the Industry

☆   Are there certain geographic areas where work of this kind is more or less plentiful than in others?

☆   What are the basic prerequisites for gaining employment in this field?

☆   What's the current demand for people in this field?

☆   How does this field tend to pay, compared with other sectors and kinds of jobs?

☆   What training or development do companies in this field generally provide? On what factors are performance evaluations based?

☆   What are the most desired skills, abilities and personal qualities in this field?

☆   How receptive does this sector, industry or field tend to be to people who previously worked in other settings?

☆   What forces do you see affecting this field or your job in the foreseeable future? New technology? Government regulation? Changing competition? Changes in the way work is structured? Changes in the work force?

☆   What are the most common problems or issues confronting people in this field?

☆   What are the best sources for learning more? Journals? Periodicals? Conferences? Associations? Who are the best kinds of people to network with, to learn all I can about this field?

Where Might I Fit In?

☆   Given your understanding of my skills and background, how good are my chances of making a successful transition into this field?

☆   What barriers would I have to overcome to make the transition?

☆   What entry-level opportunities are common in this field?

☆   What, if any, new technical credentials do you think I'd need to move into this field?

☆   What are the most effective techniques for obtaining work in this field? Are there any particular companies or employers you feel would be good targets for my efforts?

How Much Structure?

If you can memorize all these networking questions, remember them under the pressure of a meeting with a stranger, and then, after the meeting, recall all the answers given, you're blessed with formidable mental powers. Many networkers, particularly after they have had a few meetings, find it sufficient to review the guidesheets before heading off to a meeting. They know that most information will come out in the give-and-take of friendly conversation. If an important question is overlooked, call the person and say, "You know, I just realized that I forgot to ask you about . . . ." As long as you're not making a backhanded request for another hour of help—this time on the phone—you'll find most contacts cordial or even pleased at the follow-up.

If you can't stand the notion that you might forget a question that would elicit some crucial gem of information, try outlining all your questions by theme on a 5 × 7 card, or bring an attractive binder with the questions clipped inside. Understand, however, that this technique will dampen the spontaneity of the conversation.

When faced with that much structure, many contacts will react with an "I'm being interviewed" mindset, sit straighter in their chairs, and begin choosing their words carefully. You may get more information, but you've diminished the rapport and personal warmth that are key to getting enthusiastic referrals to other contacts.

Many people feel it's a major bit of rudeness for someone to begin taking down their every word the moment they start to speak, especially without first asking permission. If you must jot some points down, ask: "Do you mind if I take a few notes?" Write as little as you can. A verbatim transcription makes you look as if you can't remember anything without learning aids or you may be holding the contact accountable for his every word. The room will chill quickly. Your writing will interrupt your eye contact and impede rapport (unless you're one of those people who can write while continuing to stare someone in the face, in which case you will look like a newspaper reporter and become more intimidating).

Funny, We Were Here a Minute Ago

The Q&A portion of a networking meeting tends to meander and leap about a lot. Contacts will start a thought, then be reminded of another thought; suddenly, they'll interrupt themselves—and your train of thought. Don't overcontrol the meeting if this happens. ("Will you please finish that first thought?") You may have to gently lead your contact back from a mental walkabout: "I didn't know circus clowns used hypoallergenic makeup, Stan. That's really interesting. Let me inquire just a little further, if I might, about what you were saying a moment ago regarding product development in the cosmetics industry . . . ."

It's a Matter of Time

There's one exception to the maxim that the best networking meeting usually is the least structured networking meeting. That exception pertains to the issue of time. You've promised the contact that you won't abuse the agreed-on allocation of time. After the meeting has lasted perhaps 40 minutes, you should—almost regardless of the tempo or tenor of the meeting—glance at your watch and make a minor show of concern about the elapsed time:

Oh, hey, I promised I wouldn't use up your whole morning and I want to be sensitive to the time. But there is one area in particular I'd like to explore before we close.

Pause, and wait for a cue from the contact about how to proceed. If he says, "No problem. I'm really enjoying this," and he buzzes Mrs. Carmody and says, "Hold all calls 'til we're wrapped up here," then you have license to let the discussion continue where it will. It's now the contact's responsibility to signal when it's time to wrap things up.

If the contact says something like, "Oh, thank you. I do have a luncheon engagement I need to make," that's your signal to move on to the next act and be conscious of the time from then on.

Act 4. The Name Game

In many meetings, the process of asking for and receiving names of other potential contacts will be mixed in with all the other questions and answers. If so, great! No arbitrary division of these areas of inquiry is necessary. But if the meeting is winding down and you haven't been given the identities of other people you might talk with, you have to ask for their names.

This act is botched by many networkers; they ruin the positive impression they've successfully created earlier in the meeting by asking for names as if they're asking for a gift: "Can you give me the names of other people I should talk to?" The networking contact thinks, "I've known you for only 40 minutes and you're asking me for a present?"

There are subtler, equally effective ways of getting names. You might key the request to some point made earlier and make it look like an extension of the previous conversation:

> You mentioned a friend who had enrolled in an executive MBA program. Do you think it would be helpful if I talked to her?
>
> ———
>
> Can you think of anyone else I might talk to who has team-building experience or who has done a lot of group facilitation work?
>
> ———
>
> Of the people you know who have moved from staff jobs into line management, who do you think might be most receptive to a request for a networking meeting?

A very focused way of asking for names is to ask for specific information—in this case, who are the people who hold relevant positions in a specific company or setting?

You said you started your career in employee relations at MegaBig. Who's in charge of human resources there now? Would it make sense for me to call her?

———

"Several people have mentioned Sterling Dallas at Enviro-Comp. Do you know him? Is he someone I should get to know?"

Getting Permission—Again

Once the names start coming, *ask permission* to jot them down and then jot them down correctly! It irritates many people if you start scribbling furiously in front of them before asking, "Is it OK if I just take these names down?" Keep a 5 × 7 card in your purse or jacket pocket, and make sure you get the correct spellings and genders! (Is Lee a Mr. or a Ms.?)

You may think this is silly because you won't have any trouble remembering a couple of names. Not so. Once you depart the mild stress of the networking environment, all names, locations, and pertinent facts will try to flee your fevered brain. If you haven't captured them on paper, you have only two choices: (1) lose the name of the contact forever (the prospect of which should drive you crazy), or (2) call the contact and ask, "What was the spelling of the name of the fellow at Amalgamated again?" And he'll say, "Smith. S-M-I-T-H. Smith. John Smith." Naturally, you'll feel like a dolt, and the contact's opinion of your mental acuity may drop a little.

More important is the protocol of a request to use this contact's name when extending your network to these new names. *It's a major networking sin to use someone's name to help you get a networking meeting without getting clear, unequivocal permission to do so!*

Some networkers take liberties, thinking they'll never be called to account! Their crime may be a matter of degree. If your contact says, "You know, Lauren Miller might be an interesting person to chat with," and you call Lauren to say, "Max Jablonski said that I should call you and that you would see me," Max has a right to go ballistic toward you when Lauren calls to chide him for siccing an aggressive and presumptuous jerk on her.

When asking permission to drop the contact's name, don't make a common vocabulary mistake by saying, "Swell. I'll give Bill a call. When I do, may I use you as a *reference?*" Wrong word. A reference is a voucher, a statement of personal support. After knowing you for about an hour, your contact has no reason to offer a reference. The appropriate word is *referral*—a very different concept. "May I use you as a referral?" may sound a little heavy. The request can be made less confrontational: "Bill sounds like a very valuable person to talk with, and I'll call him immediately. When I do, may I mention that we spoke?"

There may be perfectly valid reasons why the answer will be no. The contact may be familiar with another person's reputation or expertise without being personally acquainted. In such cases, the dropping of the contact's name will produce no leverage whatsoever, and you either have to go in cold (not all that daunting; headhunters do it all the time) or locate another person who is personally acquainted with the target contact and is willing to let his name be used as a referral.

In other circumstances, your contact may know the target contact but, for a variety of reasons, may be reluctant to be the referring party. "You know," your contact might say, "Joe knows all there is to know about widgets and would be a great lead, but I'm really not comfortable having my name used as an introduction. I've asked Joe for a lot of favors recently. I haven't had a chance to return many, and I don't want to put a strain on our friendship by presuming on his good offices."

An issue of confidentiality or political sensitivity may give your contact pause. If your contact expresses *any* discomfort at being identified as a referral—much less being asking to make an introduction—back off immediately. This isn't the time to press!

Helping Your Helpers

A well-intentioned contact may not only give you valuable names, but may offer to call them or write to them, introducing you and providing a personal imprimatur. The extra credibility and leverage provided by such introductions are invaluable, if they happen. In the glow of an upbeat networking meeting, your contact may get all geared up—even to grabbing the phone and trying to get through right now—and then lose momentum when the person isn't immediately available, or forget about the promise once the networking meeting with you is history.

What should you do? The key is to determine how to lean on people without making them feel that they're being leaned on. Remember the three principles of appropriate pressure:

1. Ask how the person wants to be leaned on.
2. Always express the pressure as if it's for the other person's benefit or convenience, not yours.
3. Use the word *we* a lot.

When someone says he'll make a call for you, your response should be:

Terrific! I really appreciate that, Ed. You have no idea how much a personal introduction eases the strain of meetings with someone you don't know. Look, Ed, how should we play this? I'd hate to run the risk of embarrassing you by calling Jack before you've had a chance to get in touch with him. Would it make sense for me to call you back before following up with him? When would be a good time to check in with you? Friday? Next Monday?

A similar tactic pertains when someone offers to "share your resume with a couple of friends" or "hand a bunch of 'em out at the convention." At this point, don't ask, "How do I know you'll keep your promise?" A correct response is:

That's very kind of you, JoAnne. I'll get 20 or so resumes over to you first thing in the morning. When should I check back with you to see what people's responses were and to make sure I follow up as soon as possible? I could call in a week or so, if that's OK.

If a contact shows a willingness to go above and beyond the call of duty and wants to add some of his own momentum to your efforts, it's your responsibility to make sure he keeps rolling and he sees that you're running alongside, carrying your part of the work load. You must never, deliberately or inadvertently, suggest by word or deed that because he's taking on some responsibility, you're going to slow down, relax, put your feet up and wait for him to deliver on your behalf. Suckering other people into doing your work for you may have worked for Tom Sawyer, but it won't work for you. To make some fast enemies, respond to an offer to call a few people on your behalf with, "Oh, OK. Sounds good to me. Give me a call when you're done and let me know what they say, will you?" Such presumptuousness won't go unpunished.

What to Do When the Meeting Goes Backward

It isn't unusual for a meeting to assume a direction or agenda all its own, or for a networking contact to grab the reins and gallop off in the direction he wants to go. People who are unfamiliar with networking may latch on to an idea that these meetings are primarily to provide networkers with names. That's OK with them; they stand ready to help. You arrive, sit down, and are just about to crank up your decompression and two-minute drill when the contact grabs his Rolodex from his credenza, whirls around, says, "Ready?" and then begins racing through his file, throwing out name after name, number after number.

Don't panic and don't interrupt. His agenda is not harmful or wasteful, so let him go! Grab your pencil and write down those names and phone numbers. Your role starts when he has whizzed from A to Z and looks up triumphantly, thinking that his work is nearly done. Gently take the reins back and guide this meeting to the rest of the basic networking agenda: (1) finding out why he thinks you should talk with each of the names he rattled off; (2) taking him through your two-minute drill and making sure he understands your objectives (decompression probably isn't necessary; he has already shown that he knows you're not asking him for a job); and (3) asking him questions and probing for the information you hope to get out of this meeting.

Don't be nonplussed if the contact shows a little surprise or impatience when he realizes that his duties as an "expert" aren't confined simply to dropping names. Your first step is to show gratitude for favors already conferred:

Heavens, Bill! What an abundance of riches! If everyone were as generous with the names of possible contacts, this job search would be done yesterday. Just so I make the best possible use of these leads, would it be OK if we go back over them quickly so that I can ask why you think they'd be useful or what sort of information I should ask from them?

Warning: Don't belabor this activity. The contact has shown you his idea of the proper pace for this meeting, and you should try to keep up that pace. Once you've jotted some shorthand notes next to each name, touch on your other agenda elements:

Bill, in addition to getting the names of people with whom I can extend my network, one of the things I'm hoping to do with these meetings is to get as much job market exposure as I can and try to make sure that the people I see come away with a clear idea of who I am. If I may, let me take just a second to give you a thumbnail sketch of my background and where I'd like to go next.

When it comes to Q&A, you may want to abbreviate the give-and-take a bit. Choose three or four of the most fundamental or important issues you want to explore, and "laundry list" them, letting the contact know that this meeting isn't going to go on forever:

Bill, before we close, there were a couple of specific points I would very much value your opinion on: how much you think a Master's degree in Public Health would help me in getting an administrative job in managed care; whether my background in running a 21-operating-room suite in a 1,000-bed acute care hospital would help or hinder my getting involved in running outpatient and ambulatory care programs; and whether you think I ought to take some courses or get some training in health care finance.

Act 5. Closing Up and Getting Out

When someone asked vertically endowed Abe Lincoln how long a man's legs should be, he said, "Just long enough to reach the ground." The same is true with a networking meeting: when you've completed the agenda, take the initiative to bring things to a close. When it's done, it's done; you don't gain anything, and you can lose a lot of goodwill, by lapsing into small talk, digging into your supply of ribald jokes, or otherwise overstaying your welcome. A shy or scrupulously polite contact may have trouble telling you, "Hey, we're done. Get out of here." It's up to you to initiate closure:

> Fred, this has been most helpful. We've certainly worked through the areas I wanted to cover, unless I'm forgetting something. If so, would it be OK if I gave you a quick call with a specific question? In any event, I'm most grateful for your help, and I certainly will keep you posted on how things go from here. Oh, would it serve any purpose at all if I left a copy of my resume with you?

What about the Resume?

Until now, there has been no discussion of how to use your resume in a typical networking meeting. This was a deliberate omission. What you're trying to do in a networking meeting is to show the person, not the resume. Generally, you can do a far better job of building rapport and creating a positive impact through conversation then you can with even the most elegantly crafted resume.

Remember that a resume is a sales brochure and this isn't supposed to be a sales meeting. As discussed in Chapter 4, you may have already forwarded your resume when you confirmed the meeting, but not without decompressing the resume enclosure: "In anticipation of our meeting, I've enclosed a copy of my resume, just to give you a little better feeling for my career history and background."

Too many networkers begin meetings by saying, "Well, I guess I should give you a copy of my resume first." The contact says, "That would be good." (What else is he supposed to say? "No, don't give me your resume"?) Using your resume as an ice-breaker creates distinct problems for both the form and the content of a good meeting.

While the contact reads your resume—typically, a two- to three-minute process—you're obliged to sit there passively and silently. You may not speak, because that might ruin the contact's train of thought, which is rude. Three minutes of silence is pure hell. Being in a position where you aren't allowed to speak at the beginning of a meeting that you initiated and are supposed to drive can be incredibly unempowering. It starts you off in a passive, subordinate posture that can erode your ability to converse confidently for the rest of the meeting.

Everyone in the world fancies himself a great authority on resumes and will be pleased to pick apart yours and spend the entire meeting telling you what to do to fix it. Not only is that a downer, it's not the proper subject of this meeting, and much of this "expert" advice on resumes will be opinionated, wrong, or no better informed than your own. Letting contacts serve as resume critics relieves them of the responsibility to provide you with other forms of more thoughtful help. You need exposure, information and names, not a resume review session.

Have a couple of copies of your resume with you, perhaps in your attaché case or tucked neatly and inconspicuously in a manila file folder. If you make it to the closure of the meeting without being asked to produce it—as we did in working through Acts 1 through 5 in this chapter—great! Produce it at the end and ask whether the contact could use a copy, implying that it will serve to "lock in" the information and impression you've already made.

If, at any time in the meeting, the contact asks whether you have a copy of your resume with you, you should acknowledge that you do but suggest that the best course may be for the contact to peruse it later. If the contact persists, demur and cough up your paper. Once it's out on the table, you can use it as a "visual aid" to your two-minute drill, pointing to specific roles, settings, or accomplishments you want to highlight. On occasion, if you've provided the contact with a resume before the meeting, he'll have it in front of him when the meeting starts and will cross-examine you point-for-point about its contents. If that happens, grin and bear it; at least the contact has already seen it and you don't have to suffer in silence while he reads it through.

Act 6. The Follow-Up

You're outside the building again! You did fine. The meeting had a nice pace, and the contact's body language expressed interest and enthusiasm. You didn't make any horrendous mistakes and you projected focus and confidence. You got a few potentially valuable names *and* the contact's promise to make some personal introductions later.

But you're not done yet. After the meeting, one brief but extremely important step remains: the follow-up. No smirks or yawns here, please. This isn't the thank-you note your mom told you to write your Aunt Minnie to thank her for your birthday suit.

An implicit promise underlies all networking meetings: *If you give me a little of your precious time, I'll guarantee you the satisfaction of having helped me.* This pitch, you will recall, is aimed at the universal human urge toward empowerment. Merely saying thank-you at the close of the meeting probably isn't enough to satisfy your guarantee. Drop the contact a brief thank-you note—handwritten if your writing is legible—*after you've acted on any single suggestion or bit of advice the contact provided.* Notice how smoothly an I-took-your-advice item is worked into this letter:

Dear Nora:

Thanks once again for taking time out of your busy schedule to see me on Tuesday. Your thoughts on discount merchandising of maternity outfits were particularly helpful, and your suggestion that I talk with Leo Kohlski proved an incredible door opener. I've already met with Leo, who immediately introduced me to his three partners, and they say they can get me a booth at next month's trade show. Outstanding! A major break.

I'll certainly keep you posted, both on what happens at the trade show and on my progress generally. If I can ever return the favor in any way, please don't hesitate to call.

Sincerely,

Susan Wells

This innocuous-sounding note has carried a ton of freight. The contact has the satisfaction of knowing that she's been of help. She may be impressed by how promptly and actively you pursued her suggestion and by your initiative. Finally, you've adroitly laid the groundwork for periodic future follow-up calls to see whether the contact has heard or learned, since the meeting, anything new that is of value to you. The cost–benefit ratio for the five minutes it takes to direct a post-meeting follow-up note to each contact is extraordinarily high.

People who feel that their urge to help has been exploited are a major source of the bad-mouthing that networking receives. Too many networkers never take the time to thank the contact promptly after a meeting or to follow up with information on the progress or outcome of their job search efforts. A general manager of a consulting firm complained:

Who needs this? If networkers don't have the courtesy to thank me for my time or the sense to check back with me, they can count on my having some unkind things to say about them if their name ever comes up in conversation. I have a long memory for inconsideration. I don't get mad. But I do get disappointed. And believe me, I do get even.

This chapter has described the typical, classic networking meeting. Probably none of yours will follow this agenda exactly, but the basic model will reassure you over and over again.

FOR YOUR INFORMATION

NETWORKING MEETINGS ARE WORTH THE EFFORT

The networking meeting is an art form. Practice and repetition are required to perfect your style. Once you master it, you will:

☆ Be confident and comfortable in your self-presentation; no glitch, misunderstanding or difficult contact will throw you off stride.

☆ Be able to articulate a focused and succinct job search or career development goal.

☆ Have ruled out a lot of roles and directions that have no promise for you.

☆ Have acquired a lot of information. Some of it will be useless or wrong, some will be interesting, and some will give you a clear sense of direction in your job search.

☆ Have learned of several interesting opportunities.

☆ Have a lot of people with their antennas turned to your channel, absorbing information that they can pass along to you.

☆ Have made new friendships that will long survive your job search.

☆ Have a greater sense of personal control than you ever imagined.

6

Where Good Vibes Come From

Successful networking goes beyond merely showing your flag to a passive audience; it's about building rapport: getting people to know you, to like you, to identify with you and to go to bat for you. Because rapport is rooted deeply in the subjective depths of human nature, there's often no way of telling who will turn on to you or be turned off by you. You can't compel or instruct people to like you. You can only give them the raw materials and let their natural inclinations take over from there.

Building rapport is not an utterly hit-or-miss proposition. It has some elements of relationship building that we can discuss here without forcing you to wade through a lengthy psychological treatise. But there are some unknowable and imperceptible factors in being liked; to some extent, people simply like whom they like and help whom they want to help.

Let's look at some elements that you can master in order to promote a constructive, energized rapport on the part of your networking contacts.

The Short Version

Even if you have an innate distaste for discussions of "touchy-feely stuff" or are so confident of your natural warmth, self-presentation skills or charisma that you feel little need for supplemental instruction, at least skim this chapter and memorize the briefest of its precepts: Rapport is a function of 2 Fs: Focus and Friendliness. Focus you should have down pat. (That's what Chapter 2 was all about.) If you're unable to project a clear focus right now, you will after you've had five or six networking meetings.

Friendliness, in this context, builds on the Golden Rule: You'll tend to get what you give. Be open, and your contacts will be open. Be considerate, and they'll be considerate. Be helpful and eager to please, and they'll respond in kind.

There's no requirement that you be a smooth, silver-tongued orator or a natural salesperson. Successful networking doesn't hinge on your giving a series of dazzling performances. If you get tongue-tied, lose your place or occasionally miss the point, no one dies. If you can learn to laugh at yourself and comment candidly on your awkwardness, you have nothing to fear in a networking meeting. Go forth and have some fun.

The Words and the Music

All interactions between people have two major components: (1) manifest content—observable external behaviors and responses and (2) latent content—unspoken and often unconscious undercurrents of a transaction. For our purposes, we call them the words and the music.

Chapter 2 was all about the words; its discussion of "fit" emphasized self-definition and the ability to communicate that definition lucidly. Here we will talk about "fit" in the broader sense of understanding what factors contribute to other people's:

☆ Believing you (credibility).

☆ Respecting you (authority).

☆ Feeling they are like you (affiliation).

☆ Feeling comfortable with you (likability).

Before we look at the traits and techniques that support these desirable impressions, let's pay homage to an ability you probably aren't even aware you have.

Playing Your Hunches

Basic "hunch theory" proclaims that, in any interpersonal transaction, you'll feel comfortable as long as the words and music are in harmony. The moment they diverge and begin to send different messages, you'll note and feel and sense that something isn't quite right. As you network, it's wise to learn to admit and take note of that feeling. It's a signal that things aren't exactly as they seem.

Have you ever had the feeling, in an otherwise pleasant conversation, that something suddenly has gone wrong? Trust that it has. Or that you've lost the other person? You have. Or that the person suddenly has stopped buying your act? In all likelihood, that's exactly what has happened.

Your hunches are usually right. They're the product of sophisticated perceptual and evaluative faculties you don't use consciously. Overrule your magnificent natural hunch-making ability too blithely, and you'll cripple your judgment. The rational left side of your brain provides law and order, but the right side is your tuning fork, your dowser, your diviner of unseen facts and forces.

From birth, your biologically driven urge to survive has led you to develop ways of distinguishing warm, happy things from cold, dangerous things. Before you could talk or make logical deductions, your powers of observation were drawing a remarkably acute, ongoing map of your world. This process became second nature. Even after you "grew up," cultivated your rational faculties, and imposed conscious reason on everything, your amazing preconscious radar continued—and still continues—to work. It monitors and evaluates the myriad messages sent by the people in your surroundings.

It's easy to miscommunicate deliberately—that is, to lie—with words. But because most of us can't control a large part of the music we radiate, it's harder to distort that part of the message in order to deceive or cover up. This is true of both parties in a networking meeting, whether they are sending or receiving.

Knowing how your hunches work isn't as important as knowing that they exist. Of the many books on body language, transactional contextual analysis, kinesics and gestalt theory that crowd self-help bookstore shelves, few are of much practical utility to you. They may make interesting reading for PhDs, but they

FOR YOUR INFORMATION

LOOK BEYOND THE WORDS

Experts in kinesics—the science of body language and nonverbal communication—suggest that, in any face-to-face meeting, more than half of the total message content is conveyed nonverbally. Two people chatting are bombarding each other with an array of intended and unintended cues that serve as potential signals about how to read the situation. Some, like a blush, are readily apparent to the observer. Others, like breathing rhythm, changes in muscle tension or pupil dilation, are more subtle and may not even be consciously perceived by the other person.

hardly serve as field manuals for building rapport. Indeed, many of these books actually impede the spontaneity of communications by asking you to focus on a level of intuition that usually operates automatically. Many "formula" books suggest that you become very self-conscious—and other-conscious, too. They suggest that you learn a "hidden vocabulary" so that you can bend every interaction to your will. Some state that literally every gesture, tic, or sigh has its own unique meaning and demands decoding. ("Her pupils just dilated! I wonder what that signals!")

This is simply wrong. The nonverbal communication that's the basis of our "hunches" tends to be structured around "constellations" of messages, some of which we're conscious of and can control (posture, dress, and personal hygiene), some of which we can control if we concentrate on them (gestures, use of space, eye contact, rate of speaking), and some of which operate either automatically or unconsciously (blushing, pupil dilation, coloring, muscle tone, timbre of voice, sweating, basic gestural style). No single element acts alone; our style and the impressions of confidence, authority, anxiety or fear that we convey contribute to the total of our many cues and signals.

If you try to control particular elements of your nonverbal presentation, you run two risks:

1. When you try to balance your attention between manifest and latent content, you're likely to look self-conscious. It's difficult to operate on two channels at once, and people who are trying to change some part of their natural style often appear detached, awkward, unfocused, or self-conscious. Psychologists have a name for this: "inappropriate affect." Your contact is more likely to call it "weird."

2. Your contacts, who are themselves sophisticated receivers of nonverbal signals, may feel that they're being manipulated when you pointedly cross your arms and lean back or encroach across the midpoint of their desks. They won't enjoy being sucked into an unspoken power struggle, and the meeting will either ramble off track or become a battle of wills.

When networking, it's far more important to appear focused, attentive, and interested than it is to keep yourself on the alert for sudden pupil dilation. Leave your hunches to their own devices. Nature set it up that way, and the arrangement serves you well without your trying to overcontrol or intellectualize it.

When you detect a sudden disharmony between the words and the music, don't override your intuition. Try to pinpoint the moment you became aware of that funny feeling and to recall what happened just at that moment. If there's no obvious reason for a sudden change in someone's demeanor (like when you said, "You trying to make a statement with that tie, Herb?"), you can try a quick "reality check." Here are some examples:

> Marv, I may be wrong, but you seem uncomfortable with my explanation about why I left Amalgamated. Does that need some clarification?
> ───────
> Susan, you look perplexed. Maybe I should rephrase that last point.
> ───────
> I sense that my response may have irritated you, Herman, and I'm not sure why. I didn't intend to be cavalier. Have I touched a nerve?

If your attempt at damage control is done politely and sincerely, the other person often will tell you what signal is causing the reaction. If the meeting is threatening to jump the tracks, your candor may save the day.

The Eyes Have It (So Watch Your Mouth)

There are two noteworthy exceptions to the basic idea that you should just be yourself and let your natural style find free expression: (1) eye contact and (2) rate of speech. In our culture, "the eyes are the window to the soul." Strong, solid eye contact conveys candor and trust (in some other cultures, lowered eyes are a signal of deference, not shame or an attempt to hide the truth). Most people tend to break eye contact when thinking, then reestablish it when speaking or listening. But too many of us are shy or have gotten lazy in our habits: in a conversation, we tend to spend more time out of eye contact than in it, creating an impression of either evasiveness or a lack of interest.

You can improve your eye contact simply by forcing yourself to think about it. It's a behavior that you can modify over time until it becomes natural to engage eye contact more strongly, or until you've mastered the knack of looking natural as you consciously remind yourself to spend more time staring into someone's eyeballs. (If looking into someone's eyes makes you too uncomfortable, try focusing on the bridge of the nose; it works almost as well.) Networking meetings probably aren't the best places to practice; until you've mastered this new behavior, you're apt to be inconsistent in your eye contact, which will unnerve the people you're meeting with. Practice during regular day-to-day interactions where nothing is at stake.

Hello, Motor-Mouth

Your rate of speech may not be something you're terribly aware of, but those listening to you are. Under the stress of a networking meeting (you're being judged, you are responsible for maintaining the pace, and you must keep within agreed-on time constraints), you might speak faster than normal, run sentences together, and breathe on the fly in rapid, sucking gasps. This is called "pressured speech." In addition to betraying nervousness and a lack of self-confidence, your delivery may give contacts the impression that they shouldn't interrupt your torrent of words. They won't; they'll let you keep talking. You, in turn, won't understand why they're so silent, which will make you more nervous, which will make you talk still faster until you find yourself overcontrolling the meeting with your speech rate.

Under networking pressures, many people lapse into "interrogatory inflection": the pitch of their voice tends to rise sharply at the end of almost every phrase or sentence. It sounds like they're asking a series of questions, and it's the way eight-year-olds tend to talk. If you want to "hear" what it sounds like, just read the following aloud:

> Um, I was born just north of Chicago? My Dad was a CPA who wanted me to join him in his firm? I went to parochial high school and then to Valparaiso College in Indiana? I found I was not good at math? So I majored in political science? I graduated summa cum laude? So I got into Columbia? After I got my PhD in 1983, I joined the State Department?

In an adult, this speech pattern conveys a lack of confidence. It implies such concerns as: How'm I doing? Does this make sense? Do you believe me? Am I

FOR YOUR INFORMATION

SLOW DOWN

Trial lawyers and news announcers use a good technique for slowing speech and sounding more confident. To practice it, drop the pitch (not the volume) of your voice distinctly at the end of each phrase or sentence. Pause briefly. Breathe. Start speaking again. You'll find that you can speak very quickly between pauses without sounding rushed. With a little practice, this speak-drop pitch-pause-breathe-speak pattern can become second nature.

talking too much? Do you like me? It also tends to make all phrases equal; important points sound just like incidental points. Talk this way and you'll sound as if you're not interested in your own conversation.

Lights, Camera, . . .

Speech and eye contact patterns show up readily on video. If you have any qualms about your style, put your camcorder on a tripod facing you as you face and talk to a family member or friend. Have a ten-minute conversation (you'll need the first five minutes just to forget the camera is recording your every move) that includes your two-minute drill, your tale, and your objectives. Play it back at regular speed first. Look for patterns of eye contact and listen to the timbre and rate of your speech. Then rewind it and play it through on fast-forward, looking particularly at your hand gestures and posture. If your hands are in constant motion, dart around, are too theatrical (this usually means they fly out past your body plane), resemble a hummingbird in flight, or include nervous patterns (tapping fingers, playing with glasses or pencils and so on), the high-speed playback will make this very clear.

In real life, your hands and habits may be distracting. The best way to quiet such mannerisms is to become calm and confident about who you are and what you're doing. Working piecemeal to correct specific mannerisms is tough and often unproductive. It may make you look like a talking dog.

Whom Do You Like?

Let's return to credibility, authority, affiliation and likeability. This last attribute builds on the first three. Whom do people like? First and foremost, they like people who make them comfortable. OK, you say, but what makes them comfortable?

Ask that question of a potential employer, and the first thing he'll say is, "What makes me comfortable is solid evidence that a potential employee really is capable of adding the value I'm going to pay him for." Because you're not selling anything to a networking contact, his first response is, "I'm most comfortable with people who are like me." The next question is, then, what does "like me" mean?

It means that you share a general value system, defined broadly as the set of norms and values you support. The private sector in the United States, for example, generally adheres to the upper-middle-income value system, which places a high premium on hard work, results, team play, and aspiration for greater authority, visibility and status—all frequently measured in terms of dollars and earning power. This value set is strongly anchored in a pressure toward conformity.

The nonprofit sector's hub is providing service or adding values to other human beings. Income maximization is secondary to other measures of worth; collaboration and team play are accorded high priority. This value set is anchored in norms of affiliation and community.

The academic sector values the attainment of knowledge and understanding, is willing to forego some earning capacity in exchange for the thrill of enlightenment (and imparting that knowledge to others), and tends to reward individual, autonomous exploration more than the other value systems do. Its value anchor tends to be individuality.

Each of these broad value systems recognizes the existence and worth of the other systems, but regards its own system as being "better."

Showing sensitivity to the diversity of other people's hot buttons doesn't require you to become a boot-licking sycophant or a chameleon; integrity is essential to successful self-presentation in any setting. But you should be attuned to and respectful of the values of your networking contact, even if they're not your own. If you condescend to your contact or show disdain for something he cares about—his bowling trophy, his pair of matched Purdy over-and-under shotguns, his Volunteer of the Year award or the software program he created himself—he'll take offense, become defensive and decline to provide you with any meaningful help.

On the upside, people with similar operative values tend to like each other and develop rapport quickly and easily. This helps explain why some meetings develop a splendid momentum while others just clunk along. When you need to

---

FOR YOUR INFORMATION

UNDERSTANDING VALUE SYSTEMS

As part of each person's general value system is one specific operative value or personal priority that he or she weighs most heavily. Edgar H. Schein, author of *Career Anchors: Discovering Your Real Values* (1990, University Press), describes eight broad categories of these priority values and suggests that, in most people, one is strongly dominant (he calls it the "career anchor") and may be supported by one or two others. Schein's categories include:

1. Technical/Functional Expertise (If you want something done right, do it yourself.)
2. General Management (I like managing others to achieve organizational outcomes.)
3. Autonomy (What's most important is the freedom to do what I want in my own way.)
4. Security/Stability (I value knowing where I stand more than trying new things.)
5. Service (I want to do things that add real value to the world.)
6. Entrepreneurial Creativity (I want to create an organization or enterprise that reflects my priorities, even if that involves considerable risk.)
7. Pure Challenge (The tougher the task, the better I like it.)
8. Life-style (I seek a balance among my career, my family, and my personal needs.)

For the networker, these categories translate into a fractured maxim: When in Rome, don't inadvertently demean the Romans' values.

---

collect names, you'll probably get more referrals and offers of personal support from contacts who are wired like you.

Temperament Recognition

The networker's and contact's respective values aren't the only factor affecting rapport. The basic personality style of each person you meet will have a marked impact as well. If you can understand and recognize some fundamental patterns of how people learn and understand, make decisions and relate with others and the environment, you'll be better equipped to foster rapport and consistently produce constructive encounters.

Among the many instruments that measure these patterns is one we've mentioned often: the Myers–Briggs Type Indicator (MBTI). This instrument measures people's psychological preferences (their comfort level with various kinds of people, situations, and activities) using four scales:

1. Extrovert–Introvert (in short, outgoing and affiliative vs. self-energized and autonomous);
2. Sensor–Intuitor (learn and understand by processing here-and-now details vs. thinking in terms of concepts, theories and future possibilities);
3. Thinker–Feeler (make decisions rationally and logically vs. subjectively and emotionally);
4. Judger–Perceiver (results-oriented vs. experience- or discovery-oriented).

One respected clinical psychologist, David Keirsey, in elaborating on the sixteen possible MBTI types (or perhaps committing heresy, depending on how you look at it), developed a "shorthand" model that distills personal traits and preferences down to four broad stereotypic temperamental groups. Getting a grasp on these broad tendencies can help you understand a lot about the preferences and predispositions of the person you're networking with (as long as you realize that there are a lot of other factors that affect rapport besides basic temperamental style).

According to Keirsey, the general population (at least of the United States) breaks into four basic groups:

1. NFs (Intuitive Feelers)
2. NTs (Intuitive Thinkers)
3. SJs (Sensing Judgers)
4. SPs (Sensing Perceivers)

Because the four types are not distributed evenly throughout the population, you're much more likely, during the course of your networking, to encounter some types more than others. About 12 percent of us seem to be NFs and perhaps a like percentage are NTs, although that percentage rises dramatically when college-level education is factored in. SPs represent perhaps 35 percent overall (the percentage drops when college education is factored in, suggesting that this type is socioeconomically determined), and fully 40 percent of us will look and act like SJs.

As we take a brief look at these four types, remember that we're casting them as broad and extreme stereotypes that are exaggerated for the sake of illustration. No one, for example, is completely and totally encompassed in the SJ stereotype, but a lot of people will express a clear preference for SJ-like traits, settings and people over other types. (See Table 6.1.)

NFs: Upbeat, big picture, intensely personal

NFs are what other, less affective types tend to label as "touchy-feelers." Their lives and their work focus are strongly on human beings, human values, and the process of personal growth and self-actualization. Clear NF types usually aren't hard to spot. When you walk into the office of an NF, the surroundings—lots of pictures, snapshots of the family, plaques, prizes and knick-knacks, a disheveled desk and some evident chaos and disorganization—will proclaim: "I'm a human being! I'm an individual! I want you to know and understand me."

NFs are "people people." They tend to be empathetic, friendly, and helpful in all things, including networking meetings. They motivate others, put themselves out for others, and tend to take on responsibility for others' well-being.

NFs are excited by career change: they support and reinforce the desirability of constant growth, constant movement, and new challenges. When the rest of the world seems to be telling you "No," they'll be pitching for you and urging you on!! (NFs use two exclamation points to add an extra *oomph!* to life.)

Your meetings with NFs will be fun and upbeat, but there are a few caveats when soliciting their advice and cultivating their friendship. NFs sometimes aren't the greatest reality testers or the most objective sounding boards of what's feasible and what isn't. Their enthusiasm is infectious, but their tendency to think and understand things at a highly abstract level means that the details of actually implementing your career change may get short shrift. This is why there are many more NFs in "staff" positions than in "line" or general management jobs. They frequently are much better at envisioning and focusing on process than at producing results; their focus is more on means than on ends.

NFs see everything intensely personally. Because they have a highly subjective view of the world, their enthusiasm sparks easily and their feelings get hurt easily. If they're left out, demeaned, or not taken seriously, they can hold a grudge that they'll trot out every time the offender's name is mentioned. Be very careful of NFs' feelings. Respect them, respect their time, respect their priorities. NFs tend

Table 6.1   Temperamental Styles

	NF (Intuitive Feeler)	NT (Intuitive Thinker)	SJ (Sensing Judger)	SP (Sensing Perceiver)
Primary motivators	Self-awareness, insight, growth	Mastery, expertise, challenge	Organizational Identity and affiliation	Action and experience
Best role	Facilitator/Motivator	Visionary, innovator, system builder	Manager, planner, decision maker	Troubleshooter
Style	People-oriented, empathizes	Concept-oriented, logical, autonomous	Results-oriented, decisive, organized	"Just do it"
Adverse factors	Personalizes, not results-oriented	Not a team player, quibbles	Inflexible, critical, conservative	Impulsive, bored easily, low follow-through
Pathways	Powerful people motivators, empathic, aware of others feelings, powerful persuaders authority in self-awareness	Powerful conceptualizers, system planners, competent and consistent, firm-minded and fair, authority is in being competent, the "expert"	Powerful administrators, precise, decisive, take charge, hold subordinates/system accountable, don't reward expected behavior; authority is in organization/ system	Flexible problem solvers, immediate/ resourceful, grounded/hands on, quick starters "Ready, fire, aim."
Pitfalls	Personalize; hold grudges, carry/ rescue everybody, Guilt-ridden Conflict adverse Emphasize means over ends	Mental gymnastics/ game players/ trivializers, Not detail-oriented, complex and theoretical—cannot give a simple answer, Impersonal and detached, not team players	Nit pickers, inflexible; resist change, conservative, see the negative, not the positive, upward accountability, "The boss [or the system] made me do it"	Can create problems when none to solve, lacks foresight, gets bored easily, low follow-through, resists authority, autonomous

to be conflict-averse, so they won't tell you you're doing something wrong—in the networking meeting or elsewhere—and they may be reluctant to rain on your parade or be up-front in suggesting that your career objectives are utterly impossible.

NTs: What's your theory and how will you do it?

Like NFs, the NT temperament type wants and needs to understand, but that's not enough. NTs are visionaries and creators, but their natural penchant for theory and design extends to how to translate theory into action and measurable outcomes. As Tables 6.1 and 6.2 suggest, NTs are turned on by competency and the mastery of new skills and knowledge. Ask an NT whom he respects most, and he'll say, "I respect people who are good at what they do. Good intentions and grand dreams are nice, but what really counts is achievement. How are you going to get the power to the road?"

NTs have little need to share their personal psychology with anyone, and their rational nature may make them seem aloof and distant. You can capture their imagination, if not their hearts, with well-conceived visions, concepts and strategies. They are idea people. When encountering a career changer, they lean toward neither indiscriminate enthusiasm nor cautious pessimism. They'll want to understand your theory ("Why are you making this career move? Why now?") and your plans for translating that theory into action. It's in translating concepts into reality that they can be of most help. They love to be asked, "How did you do it?" and to give advice about creating action plans, setting priorities and measuring results.

NTs tend to embrace mastering new challenges, not stability and security. Indeed, one problem they often have is that even the most significant achievements fail to motivate them for long; their psyche is forever nagging, "What's next?" Accordingly, they tend to be quite comfortable with change and often progress through a lot of different jobs and roles during their careers. Thus, they're good networking resources for career changers, provided the networker comes to them with some sense of direction.

NTs don't personalize, the way NFs often do. NTs' frame of reference is rational, logical and objective. They tend to be truth-tellers, often to the point of being blunt and perhaps insensitive to others' feelings. You can always tell an NT by the frequent use of two phrases: "That doesn't make any sense" and "I don't understand." For reality-testing, NTs probably are the most valuable of networking contacts, because they won't soft-soap you or rain on your parade simply because you may be different from them. Because they aren't conformists by nature, their offices may show a stronger emphasis on design and individuality than on

Table 6.2   Comparative Styles

	LEADERSHIP STYLES	TEACHING STYLES	LEARNING STYLES
NF	Searches for meaning and authenticity Empathetic Sees possibilities of institutions and people Communicates appreciation, enthusiasm, approval Highly responsive to interpersonal transactions Keeps in close contact with staff Highly personalized Gives and needs strokes freely	High commitment to students Can mobilize students' talent Prefers interactional experiences to lecturing In touch with climate of classroom Relates individually to each student Accepts students and colleagues easier than superiors Prefers small group to large group Highly personal; strokes easily, tenderhearted, content	Needs acceptance, caring, support Enjoys group interaction Prefers cooperation over competition Focuses more on people than on the abstract concepts Learns best in face-to-face dialogue
NT	Hunger for competency and knowledge Works well with ideas and concepts Intrigued and challenged by riddles Sees systematic relationships Focuses on possibilities through nonpersonal analysis Likes to start projects, but not good with follow-through Not always aware of others' feelings Responsive to new ideas	Enjoys designing new curriculum Stretches students' intellects Prefers to teach knowledge rather than attitudes Does not often express appreciation Apt to be well-read in field Impatient with needless paperwork or unproductive meetings Often can sound harsh or impatient Expects competency of students and is often demanding	Interested in principles and logic Enjoys developing own ideas Finds technology appealing Needs constant success experiences Exerts constantly escalating standards on self and others Seeks to find meanings, patterns and concepts
SJ	Hungers for belonging and contributing Prizes harmony, service and tradition Orderly, dependable, realistic Understands and conserves institutional values Expects others to be realistic Supplies stability and structure	Responsible, dependable; creates harmony Presents material in sequence, well outlined Impatient with disruptive students Teaches by the Socratic method Can be critical of students who are tardy, seen disorganized, or slow	Values responsibility, dependability, obedience Prefers a structured classroom Likes and needs organization, schedule, discipline of authority Does well with workbook Values measurable outcomes

Table 6.2   (*Continued*)

LEADERSHIP STYLES	TEACHING STYLES	LEARNING STYLES
More likely to reward institutionally rather than personally (trophies, letters, etc.) Can be critical of mistakes more easily than rewarding of expected duties	Expects lessons to be done on time Loyal to organizational structure Expects students to be loyal	
SP Hungers for freedom and action Deals with realistic problems Flexible, open-minded Willing to take risks Highly flexible, adaptive Can be perceived as impulsive Challenged by "trouble spots" but not long-term Best at verbal planning and short-range projects Often strikingly innovative problem solvers	Values activity, risk, adventure Very spontaneous in classroom Does the unexpected Entertaining, attractive Not many in formal education Apt to use drama, visual aids, video tapes Tends to follow impulses rather than well-laid plans	Entertainer, free spirit, resourceful Immediacy, short attention span, spontaneity Needs physical involvement and activity Not a good team member Thrives on verbal and visual May well be restless in "regular" classroom settings "Just do it"

doing what the other folks do. They tend to like new things, modern decor, gadgets and techniques that are efficient. Thomas Jefferson was a first-rate NT. Ben Franklin wasn't bad, either.

Other than their tendency to be blunt and hyperrational, NTs have one other trait you should remember: NTs usually are enthusiastic at the start of a task or project, but their follow-through is suspect. They're better visionaries and initiators than implementers. If an NT says he'll make a few calls for you, send you copies of some abstracts, review your strategic plan, or call you at New Year's, you must take appropriate steps to ensure that these well-meant offers take place. You have to be the one to follow up and set specific agenda steps. Go ahead and lean on them; they won't take offense.

SJs: The managing majority

SJs run things. That's their bag. They take the NTs' glorious visions and implement them, manage them and drive them toward the bottom line. SJs embody the American ethos: they're rooted in here-'n'-now reality and are driven to produce tangible, measurable results. They're decisive, judgmental, orderly, control-oriented and, above all, results-oriented. They deal with the facts at hand rather than hypothesizing about abstract theories or slogging around in human emotion. There are a lot of SJs. Fully 40 percent of the people who take the Myer–Briggs Type Indicator (MBTI) test show this pragmatic results-orientation.

For SJs, individual achievement isn't as rewarding as the accomplishments of the group or the organization. They define themselves largely in terms of their teams or companies, and they tend to be strong traditionalists who value stability, status, conformity and time-honored values and techniques. Because SJs are results-oriented first, middle, and last, they spend a lot of time trying to identify and minimize anything that might impede getting results. By nature they tend to be risk-reducers, more cautious and conservative than other temperamental types.

A dyed-in-the-wool SJ may see risk in many places: in "people who have bounced around in too many jobs," in "loose cannons who are always trying to change things," in "someone with a perfectly respectable job who wants to throw it all away to go tooting around and do his own thing." SJs are natural skeptics and cynics. They get consistent results because they keep their eye on the ball, their shoulder to the wheel, their nose to the grindstone, their ear to the ground—and can somehow work productively in that position.

Conventional job seekers may fare better with SJs, or at least feel greater natural rapport with them, than career changers will. Most job seekers are pursuing linear career paths; their objective is to create an extension of what has gone before. To an SJ, this is the most prudent and least risky road, and the one with the highest probability of producing immediate results—which is the name of the game.

One SJ equated making a midlife career shift with "throwing yourself off a cliff with the hope that you'll be able to stitch together a parachute before you hit the rocks below." At midcareer, they reason, a sense of responsibility should overshadow the sense of adventure: "Don't you think it's time you settled down and grew up?" The very phrase "nontraditional career path" gives them the willies. Why would anyone want to do that? To many SJs, the decision to switch from a conventionally defined job into some new endeavor or environment represents a rejection of the SJ value system, and they tend not to take such rejection kindly.

If career changers' networking meetings with SJs are unlikely to be upbeat, they nonetheless may be extraordinarily useful. No one will reality-test your ideas as rigorously as a strong SJ; no other type is as likely to force you to examine the consequences—good and bad—of your plans and actions. For many a storm-tossed job seeker, the advice of a wise and prudent SJ is a crucial anchor, a stable point around which to orient.

SPs: Ready, fire, aim!

If you simply look at the statistics, you think you'll run into a lot of SP types in your networking: over one-third of the people who take the MBTI fit somewhere in that category. (Probably a large percentage aren't "true" SPs, but people whose preferences are socioeconomically determined. People who have to "get a job" or "go to work" often have little choice about their work lives. They have jobs, not careers. Because their work often is inherently unfulfilling, in their "spare" time they experience as much excitement as they can.)

You won't find many SPs among people who see the big picture, can make things happen, know their way around organizations or are in positions of great wisdom or authority. Why? Because they're out *experiencing* life, not trying to plan, control, or anticipate it. SPs are the inspiration for the Nike motto: "Just do it" (spoken with equal parts energy, frustration and impatience). The true SP believes that life is a huge bucket into which you dump as much sensory experience as you can until you die. They don't look for patterns or theories or plans. They look for opportunities to try things, to feel things, to juice their senses. More than 70 percent of all firefighters, for example, are SPs.

Although they tend to run in packs, SPs tend to be highly autonomous, inasmuch as sensory experience is a highly subjective and individual activity. To others, they often appear impulsive, easily bored, or unreflective. They don't much like to be asked for advice; if you want to learn from them, you follow their example: "Here's how to do it. Just do what I do." They prefer not to try to explain things in the abstract; they'll just ask you if you want to come along and try whatever activity they're doing. They won't respond well if you ask them what to do with your life. They don't want the responsibility: "Hey, do what you want. Whatever's cool. OK?"

SPs will warm to you if you show interest in their interests or in the technology they frequently use to enhance their self-stimulation. NTs and SPs often run together, because both types are always looking for new things to do (NTs, in order to master them; SPs, simply experience them). SJs and SPs don't get on well. The love of change in the SP's menu is inherently unsettling to many SJs, and not a little frivolous.

SJs often accuse SPs of being poor team players (probably a fair assessment) and of being insubordinate (unfair; SPs are *non* subordinate; the concept of teamwork doesn't register with them, and organizations tend to be perceived as confining structures rather than as solid, stable foundations for collective performance). Because they so often operate out of the mainstream, SPs tend to care less than do other types about what others think of them. They may even be openly contemptuous of people who don't want to live life in the fast lane.

To network with an SP, you've got to catch him and schedule time, neither of which is easy. SPs tend to be on the go, in constant movement, and in flux—even when they're standing still. They miss or forget appointments more than other types do; time management rarely is their strong suit. Similarly, following up with an SP can be tough: SPs don't want continuing responsibility and they usually don't care if they're part of someone else's network. But SPs can be incredibly stimulating to be around. They radiate energy and are passionate about their endeavors. In terms of networking, if they'll let you plug into them, you can really get your batteries charged.

Yes, But You're Not My Type

A strong note of warning is in order here. Approaches like Schein's, Keirsey's or the MBTI's (among others), which help identify an individual's values or operative preferences, merely enhance your ability to build a positive, constructive relationship within the confines of a brief networking encounter. They may help you to be more sensitive to what's going on in a meeting and to understand why someone reacts the way he does. But they aren't magic bullets or secret, manipulative formulas that you can use to manufacture rapport.

However well someone seems to fit any particular conceptual category, no one is solely or completely defined by such a category. If you act on the theory that All SJs are the same" or "Every NT will see things exactly the way I, an NT, see them," you're guilty of a gross abuse of process. Attempts to categorize people's preferences and comfort zones are descriptive, not prescriptive; they aren't meant to create reality, only to describe a part of it. They're best used to help fathom the complexities of interpersonal interactions, not to reduce them to simplistic labels.

Birds of a feather tend to sing and respond to similar songs, but, in nature, a whole population of various sizes, shapes and species of birds get on perfectly well together and often behave synergistically. You *can* have a perfectly pleasant and enormously productive networking meeting with someone whose background, value system, operative style and psychological preferences are dramatically different from your own.

The chemistry of any interaction may be enhanced by an underlying feeling of "Hey, we're a lot alike!", but diversity is fascinating in its own right, and many individuals are interested and stimulated by people whose lens of life is different from their own.

When it becomes evident in a networking meeting that you're seated across from someone whose wiring is profoundly different from yours, you may be tempted to ignore or gloss over the differences and pretend that you're just like the contact. After all, you're trying to build trust and possibly a longer-term friendship. You may be able to get away with this charade in the short run, but the longer the meeting goes on—and the more intimate it gets—the more likely you'll show your true stripes in one way or another.

The reason we all have operative styles is to operate within them. If your contact feels that you've been disguising your true values and preferences in an attempt to manufacture rapport, he's bound to react. "Is anything you've said true?" he'll wonder. "Did you think you could put one over on me, get my help, get introductions to my friends by misrepresenting yourself?" As you can imagine, if this happens, the meeting goes downhill pretty fast. A better course of action is to identify and call attention to clear differences in your style, worldview, and values.

Often, the best way to bridge the gap between human differences is to acknowledge them and savor them, thereby legitimizing them. Done matter-of-factly, this bridging should cause no particular discomfort:

> Ted, when you talk about how much you enjoy developing quantitative financial models, I realize we couldn't be more different on that score. I love fooling with theory and broad precepts, but numbers and quantitative things simply stop me in my tracks.

> _____

> Len, you've worked for 20 years for the same large organization, and apparently you both like it here and are effective in working in a hierarchical, structured setting. I spent a couple of years at Boeing and found that what other people felt was a nice, stable work environment always felt confining to me. When I got into smaller companies that placed a higher emphasis on working independently, I was a lot more comfortable—and I performed better.

> _____

> Myra, it seems to me that we approach training from different directions. You clearly have the human touch, and even in this meeting I sense real empathy and an eagerness to help. By nature, I think I take a more detached and objective stand toward teaching, and I wonder if you think an organization like this can comfortably accommodate such different operative styles.

The trick here is to highlight and validate your differences without suggesting that any positive or negative value judgment should be attached to those differences. You should neither patronize the other person nor knock yourself; false modesty is no more attractive than arrogant condescension. The facts are the facts: not everyone is alike, and that's all there is to it.

When You Blow It

Many networkers go through meetings as if they're walking on eggs; they gingerly tiptoe around, trying to be perfect. Their efforts at self-control are so extreme that their knuckles gleam white on the arms of the chair from which they never dare move their hands (lest they knock over the coffee). They live in terror that they'll lose their train of thought, forget the name of their last employer, or have to pause to collect their thoughts or take a second stab at answering a question.

This extreme care is counterproductive. In terms of personal presentation, it's OK to be human. As Big Bird and Mister Rogers tell us, all humans make mistakes, and nothing terrible happens when they do. Be as focused as possible, have your facts straight, and be attentive. But know that we all occasionally lose our train of thought, get distracted, spill coffee down our front, or call people by the wrong name. Nobody loses many style points for exhibiting universal human vulnerabilities.

When you make a mistake, blow your lines, get tongue-tied or have your mind go blank (not if, but when; it's going to happen sometime), acknowledge the problem rather than pretend nothing happened. If you try to cover up some gaffe, your attempt requires the other person to go along with the pretense, and both of you become uncomfortable. In such situations, a magic phrase can stabilize things and enlist the other person's empathetic tendencies: "Please bear with me."

We noted earlier in the book that there's a universal tendency toward empowerment: Ask for a little help, and you'll get a little help. The request to bear with you while you collect yourself, gather your thoughts or sponge off your tie is easy to grant, and most people will, graciously and sincerely. Here are some examples of the magic phrase and its variations:

> George, my fountain pen seems to have developed a leak, and ink is all over my fingers. I can't touch anything without smudging it up. Could you bear with me for a minute while I go down the hall and wash off my hands? And when I get back, might I borrow a pen that doesn't leak?
>
> ———
>
> Laura, I'm sorry. While you were speaking, an eagle flew by outside and I got totally distracted. Could you tell me again who the movers and shakers are at Amalgamated Mining?
>
> ———
>
> Jed, I'm going to have to ask you to bear with me today. My allergies are really kicking up, my sinuses are filled, and every time I look into the bright light from the window behind you it's like a shot to the head. If it looks like I'm not making strong eye contact, it's certainly not because I'm not interested.
>
> ———

Mr. Smithers, I know you've repeated it twice, but I have to confess that I still don't understand your question. I'm sorry if it appears that I'm hopelessly thick, but I'd still rather ask you to clarify your point then pretend I understand what you're driving at and try to bluff through an unresponsive answer.

War Story: No murder in the courtroom

An inexperienced young trial lawyer stood at the podium before a notoriously tyrannical judge. The lawyer was methodically cross-examining a witness in excruciatingly boring detail from a lengthy outline. "On page 14 . . . . On page 15 . . . . On page 16 . . ." he chugged along, determined not to betray his anxiety. The jury regarded him with boredom and contempt; he could tell they thought he was a tightly wrapped perfectionist. But he didn't dare relax. On he plodded: "On page 27 . . . . On page 28 . . . . On page 41! Page 41?" He suddenly realized that more than 10 pages of the outline were missing!

Thunderstruck, he lurched back from the podium and, without thinking, croaked up at the forbidding presence in black: "Judge [not "Your Honor" or "May it please the Court"], my notes just went from page 28 to page 41. Could you bear with me a second while I get my act together?" The judge paused and then softened: "Of course, Counsel. It happens to the best of us. Ladies and gentlemen of the jury, why don't we take a brief recess while the defense counsel, ah, 'gets his act together.'" Miracle of miracles, the judge hadn't held him in contempt or ridicule him! Better yet, when the jury filed in from the recess, he noticed that a few of them smiled at him and one shrugged knowingly.

He realized he had just gone from being a blue-suited bore to a fallible, likable human being. He relaxed, then the jury relaxed. It was a lesson he never forgot.

Wrecking Rapport

Unfortunately, not all human networking sins go unpunished. Some miscues aren't the result of forgivable foibles; they stem from indifference, inattention, inflexibility and indolence. They immediately and often permanently ruin any chance of a lasting rapport.

Tardiness, for example, is inexcusable. Never be late! You've asked for "a little time," yet your behavior shows that you're careless about the contact's schedule. In their rush to line up as many meetings as possible, many networkers cut the margins too fine. If an earlier meeting goes terrifically well and therefore runs long, if there's a jackknifed tractor-trailer on the expressway, if there's no parking close by or if you discover you didn't really know how to get there, you suffer the embarrassment of having abused the contact's time.

Plan logistics far more conservatively than you think you need to. Buy a street map and actually plot the route with a colored marker. Bring extra money for parking. Have the contact's phone number handy. If you get hung up, use your car phone or duck into a booth to explain the delay and to update your estimated time of arrival.

Clothes can be another problem. This book isn't about dressing for success, but too many networkers give little thought to appropriate attire. You're showing your "game face" in networking, and you should dress the way you would for work, erring a bit on the dressed-up side. If you're meeting a person you don't know or someone of distinctly higher rank than you, show deference by dressing slightly more formally and conservatively than you might otherwise. Rapport builds on respect.

Overly casual attire suggests a casual attitude about the meeting. Dress that tries to make an individual statement—a buckskin jacket with a two-foot fringe, or a flamboyant red dress with football-player shoulderpads—suggests that creating an impression is more important than building rapport.

The basic rule for dress is: *Be remarkable unremarkably.* How you dress should suggest that you care about your appearance without fixating on it. Understatement is best. Any clothing item or accessory that says, "Look at me!" will tend to shout louder than the message you're trying to convey with your mouth. Pay extra attention to personal hygiene before heading to networking meetings. Your nails, hair, breath, facial hair and body odor are all on parade and are capable of ruining an otherwise positive image. Take nothing for granted.

One sin is committed all too often: a networker rushes into a meeting, expecting and hoping for immediate gratification and help. If he doesn't learn or receive something of value instantly, he concludes the meeting is a dud, shuts down all attention systems and sits there like a lump waiting for it to end. Contacts, of course, read this "checking out" behavior. *They* can't check out—the meeting is in their office. But any perceived lack of interest on your part will be fatal to your chances of future referrals or of being remembered favorably. Even if you're bored silly by the contact's pointless or unfocused banter, you must continue to look interested. This is an art that can be mastered with practice: head nods, confirming comments ("Yes, I see." "Oh, that's interesting." "You know, I'd never thought of it that way."), and strong eye contact. Never prop your chin in your hand, examine your fingernails, yawn or sigh, or try to read anything on the contact's desk upside down. You must work hard to stay in the meeting for the whole meeting.

FOR YOUR INFORMATION

RED LIGHT, GREEN LIGHT

Following are the important underlying messages that are often conveyed in body language. Be alert for the signals!

☆ I want to talk now; please shut up for a minute.
☆ I know that already; move on.
☆ That annoys me.
☆ Not so fast! Not so fast!
☆ I don't understand what you mean, but I'm not about to admit it aloud.
☆ I find that hard to believe.
☆ That's really exciting!
☆ I really like that.
☆ We've got to begin wrapping things up.
☆ We've got to wrap things up *now!*

A final rapport wrecker is a failure to read the "red lights" and "green lights" that the contact displays during the meeting. You will have an agenda, but if you keep charging ahead without conducting some ongoing reality-checks, you may miss the contact's sigh of boredom, drumming fingers of impatience and look of confusion—all suggesting a need for clarification.

One bit of body language is pretty clear-cut: when the contact stands up (except to fetch something), the meeting is over. Close as quickly as you can, get your thank-you done pronto and promise to follow up later.

The most tragic missed signal is "running a green light"—missing some signal that your get-together has changed from a networking meeting to a meeting at which the contact is expressing interest in you as a possible employee. Some green lights are hard to miss. "What would you think about working in a place like this?" is a pretty clear indication that the person is thinking about your potential contributions to his company.

Even if you get this light, don't jump the gun by saying: "Oh? Is there a job here for me?" You'll be pushing the envelope. There's probably *not* an existing job, but a discussion might lead to the creation of a role that is custom-tailored around you. The appropriate reaction in such cases (even if you're not interested) is to express polite interest and ask the contact to elaborate on his thinking: "That's an intriguing thought, Malcolm. What kinds of needs and priorities do you have that lead you to think I might be able to make a contribution?"

Be on the alert for subtler green lights. When a contact asks you to simulate behavior or respond to a hypothetical that clearly pertains to his company, the stakes probably have changed:

> Sally, have you ever managed a sales force in a situation like we have here, where the regions operate totally autonomously of each other? How did you handle the inconsistencies in the way they used to set quotas and allocate commissions?
>
> ———
>
> Luke, I note your asset management accomplishments with some interest. We acquired a number of promising properties that may still be strong performers in the long run, but are killing us now. Did you ever face the problem of trying to balance short-term and long-term returns in a real estate market that was this unpredictable? What did you do?

When you get a green light, understand that the networking meeting has ended and your agenda has been superceded by a new agenda that the contact controls. You've moved into the twilight zone of the protointerview: you're being sized up in a different way, but you aren't in a standard screening or hiring interview where the responsibilities, stakes and authority of the job are clear.

The key here is to maintain your patience and flexibility. When you're being measured this way, just stand still and be measured. Be cooperative, responsive, and curious. Green lights often take a long time—numerous meetings over several months—to get to the "go–no go" decision point. Any opportunity is very fragile at this stage and is sustained primarily by rapport and a potential for mutual self-interest.

War Story: The death of the laser

In the late 1960s, after an early career as a corporate controller and CPA, Dale decided "to learn something about computers" in order to automate his CPA practice. He showed considerable natural aptitude: three years later he was programming moon-shot profiles for NASA under contract to a major computer manufacturer. In the following 17 years, it was recognized that Dale—a tall, quiet, rather awkward man—could create a sophisticated quantitative model to measure or describe anything.

Dale acquired the nickname "The Laser" because his managers would wheel him in, focus him on a project, and say, in effect, "Dale, zap it!" And he would, from human resources allocation studies to energy utilization projections to economic modeling to competitor analyses worldwide. He was amazing. He also was unhappy, because he never was given continuing responsibility in any of these projects. He just got wheeled on to the next project. Dale was delighted when his job was eliminated in a merger, although he was apprehensive about having to run a job search for the first time.

Because his computer skills were so esoteric, he decided his best chance was to market himself as a controller or chief financial officer (CFO) of a small or rapid-growth manufacturing business. He began networking with other CFOs, talking about opportunities in financial management. At the end of one fairly un-productive networking meeting, his contact said, "Dale, I'm sorry but I've got to go now. I'm part of a business development group that's meeting to try to figure out how to market our services in both Israel and the Middle East. We just can't figure those markets out."

"Ah," said Dale. "Very tough. I had a hard time doing that market analysis. Took forever to build a model we found reliable."

"What?!" said the contact. "Market analysis? I thought you were a financial manager."

"I can do either," Dale said agreeably. "I just thought my best shot would be as a controller or a CFO."

The contact stared at him. "Dale," he said hoarsely. "We would kill to find someone who could develop a sophisticated marketing and competitor analysis model of that area for us."

"Yeah. Well. Gee," stammered Dale. "I . . . uh . . . thought you were going to . . . uh . . . give me some names that I might call for more networking."

Stop, Do not pass Go. Do not collect anything.

What's in a Name?

As you have more and more meetings and become increasingly confident, you're going to discover a subtle dynamic: There's a mild tension between showing appro-priate deference and projecting a sense of authority and control. This is particu-larly true in meetings between men, because men tend to orient around issues of control. Women tend to be more consensus-oriented, so the issues of "who drives this meeting" usually aren't as ticklish.

One specific area where this tension shows itself is in figuring out how to address someone. Transactional analysis tells us that, in any interaction, each party tends to assume the symbolic posture of a child (passive and powerless), a parent (judgmental and directive), or an adult (rational and logical). Generally, the best meetings work adult-to-adult: each side is entitled to due deference, nei-ther side wants to assume a subordinate posture.

For networkers, this means either starting on a first-name basis or getting on one as quickly as possible. The networker already has given away a bit of power by being the one to have to ask for the meeting, and continuing to call someone "Mr. X" or "Ms. Y" only emphasizes that disparity. Where the contact is a great deal older, higher in status or more powerful than the networker, the added deference of the formal address may be called for, and reverting to a first-name basis without specific permission to do so may sound presumptuous or disrespectful.

If your age and that of the contact are within about 15 years, it's probably safe to call someone by his or her first name—indeed, many people welcome the added personalization that goes with being called by name. If the issue is in doubt, you can always ask, "Do you mind if I call you Ed?" A problem arises if Ed says, "No, I think that would be unduly familiar." Rapport is shot, you're stuck in a child–parent transaction (you've just been mildly punished for your stupidity), and the meeting is unlikely to feel very pleasant to either of you.

Accordingly, many networkers feel that the first name–last name problem is best avoided by staying away from name address altogether. Sometimes this works fine; at other times, it gets awkward at those points in the conversation—greeting, departing, expostulating, and so on—where a name usually is properly spoken. Think about this issue before going in to each meeting, figure out how you're going to play it, then be consistent.

7

Scenarios and Situations: Voices from the Front

Adult education experts know that theory doesn't translate directly to mastery. It's a long way from a solid cognitive understanding of a concept to the sense that you can put that concept to effective use, consistently and confidently. Mastery requires working through some intermediate stages: seeing the concept in action (learning by example), trying to put the concept into action under controlled circumstances (testing your wings), trial performance feedback (blowing it a few times), conscious repetition (if at first you don't succeed . . .) and, finally, integration of the knowledge into both your preconscious and your readily accessible internal database (I can do it in my sleep, but also when I'm awake).

Learning to ski, for example, requires considerable instruction before you actually *do anything*. Then you break the moves you've been shown into their component parts on the bunny hill. You watch videos of effortless masters carving flawless paths through deep powder. You compare the videotaping of your own pitiable efforts, and later spend a lot of time on the slope by yourself, visualizing and trying to imitate the mental exemplar in your head. You mess it up and try it again, all the time hoping no one will notice you.

Networking technique is no different. Although it's a common-sense process pinned solidly to the Golden Rule, networking is just different enough from the other kinds of social interaction to make you feel self-conscious and awkward—at least at the beginning and when you're confronted with the unexpected. Carrying this book with you to networking meetings and stopping the proceedings periodically to figure out what to do or say next probably won't work much better than carrying Jean-Claude Killy's *Introduction to Skiing* with you to the slope for a little on-site boning up. But inasmuch as examples tend to imprint differently on our brain from didactic prose, it may be useful at this point to listen in on some typical conversations—all completely hypothetical but rooted in situations that can happen or have happened. By eavesdropping on others, you may be able to create your own mental audio tape, parts of which may pop to mind in some real-world scene of your own. Some of these vignettes are meant to model effective technique, others to illuminate predictable pitfalls and still others to model tactical problems or issues.

Scenario 1: Starting off a career

The Setup: Ned (N) is a young man just completing the last year of a joint MBA/ JD graduate program. He has had no meaningful prior work experience, and he's not sure where and how to apply his new educational credentials. Everyone tells him he must network with people in various fields and roles to get a better sense of "what's out there." His Dad sets him up with a contact (C) who used to practice law and now runs a small food-processing company. In this first vignette, watch how quickly the failure to plan for a meeting can make the networker feel lost and defensive.

C: Well, Ned. How can I help you?

N: Dad said I should talk to you to try to figure out what to do with my career. He says I'm just drifting around and that I have to figure out what to do after I finish my joint MBA/JD.

C: Well, is he right?

N: I dunno. Maybe. Sort of. It's not like I'm just goofing off or something.

C: Tell me, Ned: what was the thinking behind undertaking such a challenging dual degree program?

N: Well, everyone said a JD would, you know, like, never hurt me. And after I started law school, I saw this posting for the joint degree program, and I just sort of thought, well, what the heck. I was good at accounting in college, so I thought I might be good at this too.

C: To what end?

N: Hunh?

C: Well, here you are acquiring all sorts of fancy tools and credentials. How do you think you're going to use them?

N: That's what Dad says I'm supposed to ask you.

C: Well, what does your Dad think I know that might be of use to you?

N: He just said you'd be good to talk to because, you know, you used to practice law and all. And then you went into business, you know, so you've sort of seen both sides of the fence.

C: Well, Ned, I'm certainly not going to take responsibility for your life, but maybe I could offer a couple of questions that might help focus your thinking.

N: Yeah, I guess that would be good.

C: Is your basic thought to use the MBA credentials to support your skills as a lawyer or to be a business lawyer with the extra expertise that comes from B-school?

N: Wow, tough question. I never really thought about it in those terms. How can I be expected to know what I want to do at my age, when I don't know all the possibilities that are out there?

C: Ned, I don't mean to sound impatient, but I'm surprised you would be investing this much time and effort in a joint-degree program and not have some idea of how you're going to use these skills. 'Well, what the heck' just doesn't come across as a focused reason for your first major career decision: what to study.

N: (Testily) Why did *you* go into law? And more to the point, why'd you leave law to go into business for yourself?

C: Those are the first decent questions you've asked, Ned, and now that we've got you warmed up a bit, let's look at my career decision-making process and see if it has any relevance to your situation . . . .

Debrief

Ned may be no more immature or anxious than others his age, and his decision to undertake a demanding joint graduate program suggests that he is, in fact, strongly goal-oriented. His problem is in his inability to *articulate* his goals, to describe the thinking that went into his decision. Indeed, in this opening exchange, he sound passive and unreflective. Several times, he suggests that the initiative for this networking meeting came primarily from his father, which suggests that his educational decision may have come from the same source. The repeated references to his father's opinion don't help Ned at all in having an adult-to-adult conversation with an older contact.

Young people or those just starting their careers often feel overpowered or tongue-tied in the presence of those who are older and more experienced in life and work. They may think their own thoughts are unworthy of credibility or respect. Note that this meeting goes nowhere until the contact goads Ned to the point where he sticks up for himself (albeit pretty awkwardly). We shouldn't expect young people to have and project a laser-beam career focus. It's OK to be young. But successful networking at this level does require them to demonstrate that they've given both their career and each networking meeting some serious thought. They must make some effort to structure issues and priorities. When networking, it's important that they be able to describe the line between what they do know—as a result of prior reflection and research—and what they don't.

Starting a Career, Take Two: Once Again, From the Top

N: Mr. Charles, I want to thank you again for taking the time to sit down with me and perhaps help me put my initial career planning into clearer focus.

C: Happy to help, Ned, but why me?

N: As you know, I'm finishing up a joint JD/MBA program next May, and although I have some basic idea of what I *could do* after graduation, believe it or not I'm not really sure about what I *want to do* . . . even down to the basic decision of whether to go into the practice of law, go for a job that could lead to management, or see if there's some kind of role I don't know about that would draw on both disciplines. I asked Dad if he knew of anyone who had experience in the practice of law and in business management, and he thought of you.

C: Well, I don't know if my example would be instructive or not.

N: I'm not sure the need is as much to make an example of you as it is to ask you about the career options and day-to-day life-style in each of the two areas—both early in one's career and later, down the road—and get your views about what factors should influence the choice of someone at my age and stage.

C: OK, but first tell me what factors led to your decision to do a joint program.

N: Actually, I started law school first, and in hindsight that may have been sort of a default decision. Becoming a lawyer certainly had the family's approval, and my LSATs were very good. And I thought the bucks and the status would be pretty good.

C: So your opinion has changed?

N: Well, at least supplemented and thought out a bit more. First of all, it's been clear to me ever since college that I might have a natural head for business. I was always real good in accounting and quantitative stuff, and I've always liked reading about business strategies and transactions. Sure beat Shakespeare for me. So, in going to law school, I wanted to emphasize corporate and business law. Do deals, set things up, play where the powerful people play.

When I saw the posting for the joint program, something about it really grabbed me. In law school, some of the courses were interesting—corporations and corporate tax, commercial transactions, contracts—but I couldn't get all that excited about being a corporate lawyer in a firm. I couldn't see spending my life just hiring my expertise out to others. I guess I wanted to be *in* a business, not just *advising* businesses. I read a lot about entrepreneurial businesses and ventures, and I guess that attracts the part of me that is both very competitive and that likes to go in new directions and do things that other people haven't done. I've got good quantitative and computer skills and thought those would probably get me farther in business than in law. So that's why I added the MBA part, to see if that would give me more leverage in getting into business. The problem is that, although I think I know where I want to end up, I'm not sure how to start. I don't know what either law or business is like in real life. That's why I thought talking to you would be particularly helpful.

C: You've clarified the issues pretty well, I think. Let me make a few generalizations about your possible choices—in law or in business—and then suggest to you what I've learned from my own experience . . . .

Debrief

Note how much better things go when Ned helps frame the issues and makes it clear that he has given his course of study and its implications some serious thought. The situation doesn't require that he have all the answers, only that he anticipate the questions and issues any helpful networking contact is bound to raise. In distinguishing what he knows from what he doesn't know, Ned makes it much easier for the contact to provide focused insights and draw relevant information from his own experience.

Scenario 2: Getting off on the wrong foot (and staying there)

The Setup: If a complete networking meeting lasts less than five minutes, something probably has gone seriously wrong. Here, in a meeting with a contact (C) who is unfamiliar with networking, Joe Job Seeker (JJS), a neophyte networker, loses control at the outset and never gets it back.

C: Hi, Joe. Nice to meet you.

JJS: Nice, uh, to meet you too. (strained silence) Well, uh, I guess I probably should show you my resume first.

C: OK. Fine by me (starts to read while Joe sits there, painfully and silently).

JJS: (Unable to bear the silence, finally speaks as C continues to read) I, uh, got your name from Ezra Blankenship over at Alpha-Zed Metals. He said you might . . . .

C: (Breaking in) Why did you leave this job? This last one?

JJS: Hunh? Oh. They had a big layoff. Lot of folks got laid off. So, uh, I . . . got laid off.

C: Did anybody stay?

JJS: Whaddya mean by that?

C: Well, if some people stayed and some people were selected for termination, how come you got the axe?

JJS: You'd have to ask those turkeys that yourself, although it was always clear that they had it in for the foundry operations group. They'd sell their own mother if it would increase the stock price.

C: (Tossing resume aside) Jeez. Too bad. These are hard times.

JJS: Yeah, well, so anyway, I'm not here looking for a job, but I was talking to Ezra, and he said you might have some names.

C: Some names?

JJS: Well, yeah. You know, of people who might know of job openings for someone like that.

C: Like what?

JJS: Oh, gosh, I guess I should tell you about my background and stuff.

C: (Taps resume) Well, I got it all. It's right here.

JJS: Well, yeah, but, I . . . you know, I'm looking for a job and . . . .

C: You are? I thought you just told me you weren't looking for a job.

JJS: Hunh? Oh, yeah, I am looking for a job. After all, I just got laid off. But I'm not here to ask *you* for a job. This certainly looks like a nice place to work, though. No, I just wanted to, ah, network with you and perhaps get some names of . . . .

C: (Interrupts) Look, Joe. I've been hearing all about this networking stuff, and that's all well and good, but there's really no one I can think of. No one I could call and say, "Hey, talk to this friend of Ezra's." I understand what you want, but there's just nothing I can do to help you out right now.

JJS: Yeah, well, I . . . .

C: Tell you what I'll do. I'll keep an eye out. Anything comes along, I'll get back to you.

JJS: That would be swell.

C: Always pleased to help.

JJS: And I'll get back to Ezra to thank him for referring me to you.

C: Yeah, well, that would be good.

Debrief

Sound farfetched? At some point or another, you'll probably experience a disaster like this. Once the locomotive jumps the tracks, it can be hard to get it back on the rails. JJS comes in unprepared to set the agenda or to reality-test C's understanding of what this meeting is all about. He hands control of the meeting over to C in the hope that C will know what's called for. The power shifts to C who, himself uncomfortable with JJS's increasing discomfort, blows JJS out as soon as he can. Every networker should expect a few meetings that go badly—but none need go this badly. If you stumble, bumble or lose momentum, *call attention to process!* Rather than pretend that nothing's wrong, acknowledge that you're confused or off on the wrong foot. Stop the action. Reset the tape. Laugh at yourself. And try for a second take ("Gosh, Moe, I don't even understand what I just said. Let me try that again in English." Or, "Jan, I clearly dropped the ball here. I should have made clear that my purpose in asking to see you was simply to do a little informal networking and not to hit you up for a job. Now that I've made that clear, would it be possible to start over from the beginning?").

Scenario 3: Blowing the tale

The Setup: During the course of a perfectly routine networking meeting, Diane (D) mentions that she "recently left Acme Widget" and the contact (C) immediately interrupts:

C: Left Acme? That's a great company! Whatever happened?

D: (Flushes; her knuckles whiten on chair arms) Well, as you may be aware, during the last several fiscal quarters, the exchange rate of the yen has vacillated through a range of over 44 percent, creating instabilities in costing and pricing that had a concomitant adverse effect on the positioning of certain products and market segments dependent on overseas component supplies. This, in turn, engendered a significant softening of domestic distributor market demand with a trickle-down impact on certain of Acme's highly elastically priced product lines. These cost and demand variables necessitated an organizational realignment, and my role was one of those impacted.

C: Oh, I see.

Debrief

In fact, the contact doesn't see. All he knows is that, when pressed on a fairly predictable question, Diane showed a lot of defensive signals: shallow breathing, white knuckles and a long, rambling and extremely abstract recitation in which Diane and her fate sounded almost like incidental players, tucked in there at the end. The contact is thinking: "Why the need to come up with an explanation that is so obviously rehearsed? Why the huge windup before the pitch? Is some damaging truth being hidden behind all the syllables? What's wrong with this picture?"

It is part of human nature *not* to acknowledge ignorance. If the contact is not following you or does not understand the technical terms or shoptalk you're using, frequently he will just keep nodding and smiling. Has the information sunk in and registered? Do the phrases "I see" and "I understand" always mean what they say? If there's any doubt, reality-test often.

Diane's Tale, Take Two

Diane will do better to put the facts in plain English, to put the punch line up front and then back and fill as needed for a simple, straightforward explanation:

C: Left Acme? That's a great company! Whatever happened?

D: Oh, Acme's in good shape generally, but my division—my job included—fell victim to the ups and downs of the exchange rate. We were introducing a new product in both U.S. and foreign markets, and we needed a lot of Japanese parts. We never knew what they'd cost, and we never knew what kind of profit we'd get when we did sell the products. The distributors backed off, and Acme took a hard look at this line and decided to cut its losses. So that was it for me and 140 other sales and marketing staff.

Debrief

Given the realities of today's workplace, being out of work is not even remotely remarkable. The fact of unemployment doesn't automatically create an assumption that you were a poor performer or are damaged goods. On the other hand, unemployed networkers must be able to articulate, clearly and credibly, the reasons for their being out of work. The tale must pass the giggle test and not jostle the hogwash meter. A simple, short and succinct tale works best.

Scenario 4: For career changers, no focus = no sale

The Setup: After several lucrative years spent selling investment-grade commercial real estate, Woody (W) has seen the real estate market collapse and his income drop from well into six figures to less than a third of that amount in the past two years. It's clearly time to make a move, and, in a sense, Woody is relieved: the money was good, but he always hated how frustrating and drawn out the negotiations were and how factors beyond his control often derailed potentially high-ticket deals. Woody, unsure of what to do next, decides to "test the waters" with a few contacts, including Clyde (C):

C: Woody! Long time, babe! What brings you to your old haunts?

W: Well, Clyde, careerwise, I think it's time for Plan B.

C: What, you mean leave RealCor?

W: I mean leave real estate. I think it's time for a new movie.

C: Oh, c'mon. Get serious. Yeah, the market's been in the dumper, but it's got to come back. Like Will Rogers said, "Buy real estate. They're not making it anymore."

W: Yeah, but they have been, Clyde. We've got such an overabundance of commercial real estate that it could be years before either the rental or sales market comes back to life. Besides, even if it did, I'm toasted, man. Bored, burnt out, battered, bummed.

C: Well, you weren't singing this sad song a couple of years ago when you were scoring the big commissions. Are you sure you're not just wimping out?

W: Get off my case, Clyde. It's my life. I'll do what I want with it.

C: Well, oooo-kay. Just what *do* you want to do with it?

W: That's the problem. I don't know what's out there. What do you think I'd be good at?

C: I think you're good at self-pity. You must be nuts, man! There is no "out there." It's just chaos, compounded by a weird economy. You've already found something you're really good at, and you want to go "find yourself"? It doesn't sound like you've thought this through. I don't see any direction, I don't see any priorities. I thought career changers were all supposed to read *What Flavor Is Your Rutabaga?* or something and do all this self-assessment. You, my friend, are a loose cannon on a wet deck, and I'm not going to help you roll over the side. You're just a little down, that's all. You don't see me leaving investment banking just because nobody's doing any big deals right now. Don't do it, Woody. Don't go off half-cocked. Have a couple of extra margaritas on the weekend and tough it through. Don't abandon your friends and throw your life away, babe.

W: Gee, Clyde, this isn't what I expected from you. I . . . I . . . really need your help.

C: You've just gotten it, man. It's called "tough love."

Debrief

Who can blame Clyde? Woody seems to be reacting, not proacting: his career change lacks focus or direction. He hasn't worked through an inventory of his strengths and transferable abilities. He sounds passive, negative, bewildered. He sounds like he's trying to get Clyde to take responsibility for deciding what Woody should do.

When people announce significant changes in their career path—particularly if they've enjoyed success or stability in their present work—it's natural for others to suspect that they're acting out or "going through the midlife crisis." To convince others to buy into and support your career change efforts, you must demonstrate that you've thought the goals through and are trying to chart toward new passages rather than simply run away from disappointment or discomfort. Many people, like Clyde, fear change. Your decision to embark on a new course may be seen as a repudiation of their values, their decision to stand pat. A career change can therefore be a lonely journey. To get others to go with you—at least in spirit—you must show determination, enthusiasm and at least a rudimentary sense of direction. Let's see if Woody can't do better.

Woody Tries It Again

W: Clydester! Hey, I've made some major decisions, and I want to bring you up to speed and get your help in putting them into effect.

C: Sounds heavy. What's up?

W: Clyde, I don't think commercial real estate sales are coming back any time soon, and I also realize I really don't care if they do. This isn't the field in which I want to spend the rest of my career in any event.

C: Gosh, Woody. I'm very surprised. When the market was up, you were making a very handsome living. You sure you're not just down because the big deals aren't dropping right now?

W: That's a fair question. One I asked myself very seriously. I don't want to go off half-cocked.

C: Then what's all this about?

W: Clyde, the money was the only thing keeping me in it. That, and I liked the fast pace of it all when the market was hot. But even before the market slowed, I was losing interest. You could do a great job on set-up and negotiation, spend months acting in good faith and trying to make constructive accommodations, and on a whim the buyers go, "So sorry, we're out. Ta-ta." And there are things other than bricks and mortar or asset management that stoke my fires.

C: Yeah, like what?

W: Well, I've looked at the parts of the job I did like, and that at least suggested some criteria I should try to address in whatever I do next.

C: Such as?

W: Well, I do like deals . . . or any kind of activity that involves getting thrown into a new situation, sizing up who's playing and what their interests are, developing a response that addresses their needs, doin' it, and moving on to another deal or program. You know me, Clyde. I like fast-paced work, and I need immediate gratification. Long-term planning or waiting five years for the payoff just isn't me. I'm comfortable meeting new people, I build trust easily with others, and—if my real estate sales record is any measure—I can be pretty persuasive.

C: So what does that leave you?

W: Well, I don't want to be just a salesman. I've been teaching beginning race drivers with the Porsche Club of America on weekends. I like motorsports, and I know there's a lot of money that changes hands in sponsorship deals. I thought my background might appeal to one of these marketing organizations or even one of the big racing teams that's always trying to secure new sponsorship bucks.

C: So that's your dream? Finding sponsors for racing cars?

W: It's worth a look—and if not racing teams, perhaps some other form of sports marketing or promotion. Several people have suggested that my deal-making background would work well there. Another friend who knows how I saved a couple of major deals that were coming unraveled said he thought I had a natural flair for what he called "crisis management"—you know, a senior manager is indicted or a product is adulterated—or even financial crises, like a hostile takeover bid or a disastrous fall in stock price. My financial skills are pretty good. That kind of troubleshooting might be a good fit.

C: That's it?

W: Clyde, the point is this: I don't expect there to be a single job or even a single industry or setting that's my one true destiny. All I'm saying is that I have a number of negotiation, persuasion, interpersonal and deal-making skills that aren't tied solely to my knowledge of commercial real estate. I'm entrepreneurial by nature, and if the country ever comes out of the recession, I'm just arrogant enough to think that some employer might find me attractive. Now, if you have any other ideas that fit this general profile, I'm certainly all ears.

Debrief

Woody is trying to get Clyde to think in terms of *categories,* not just specific job titles or industries. Often, by suggesting certain traits or aptitudes, the networker can get the contact to think a little more imaginatively. Remember: "Your friends know you only in the way they know you," and often they may resist changing the clear and comfortable image they have of you. Be prepared to lead the witness.

Scenario 5: Unsuccessful damage control

The Setup: Elmo (E) was the CFO of an entrepreneurial company that has gone down abruptly and spectacularly in flames. A front-page write-up in *The Wall*

Street Journal implied that whoever was in charge of the company's finances was either a crook or a complete incompetent. The horror story is well-known enough that Elmo already has encountered difficulties in scheduling networking meetings. On several occasions, Elmo's name hasn't registered on the contact (C) when he has called for a meeting, but the company's name rang bells at the meeting itself, with predictable consequences.

C: Nice to meet you, Elmo. How can I help you?

E: Well, Chris, my company recently went out of business, and I've been thrown into the job market. I was hoping we might do a little informal networking, with a focus on senior financial management on the Gulf Coast.

C: Fine, Elmo. I'm pretty well-connected, if I do say so myself. Happy to help. So, who were you with?

E: C. Dexter Haven.

C: C. Dexter Haven . . . that rings a . . . wait, that was the . . . Oh, Jeez.

E: Something wrong, Chris? You look pale.

C: No, no, noooo . . . .

E: Well, anyway, I know you know the lay of the land here in the South and I was thinking you might be able to suggest some . . . .

C: (Interrupting) You know, Elmo, I just realized that this may not be the best time to do this. I've got a big client meeting later this morning, and I'm really kind of preoccupied. What, ah, might make more sense is if we reschedule when I wasn't feeling quite so harried, and we could discuss your situation fully then.

E: Well, we'd only need a few minutes now, but if that would work better . . . .

C: It would, oh, yes, it would, it would.

E: Would it make sense to schedule a time now?

C: Ah, well, things are a little crazy at the moment . . . ahhh . . . why don't you get back to my secretary in a couple of days. Yes, that would be good.

E: OK, Chris. I'll follow up then. Thanks—and I hope your client meeting goes well.

C: Client meeting? Oh! Hah! Yes! *That* meeting. Yes, well, thank you and goodbye.

Debrief

There won't, of course, be any next meeting. Elmo has had no chance to explain his side of the story, to rebut the rap on him. If networking is going to work for him—indeed, if he's ever going to find appropriate work again—he has to overcome his contacts' defensiveness and at least get the issues out on the table. Doing so requires the courage to confront the issues *and* the finesse to discuss them matter-of-factly.

Elmo Breaks Through: "Validating the Aggressor"

E: Chris, I want to thank you for taking the time to sit down with me. I really appreciate your help. Particularly since, in addition to the usual challenges of trying to find a job in a tight financial management market, my situation has some particular twists to it.

C: What do you mean?

E: Ever hear of C. Dexter Haven?

C: No, I don't think I . . . wait a minute. Wasn't that the venture capital firm where the partners skimmed so much they drove it under?

E: Yup. That was my company.

C: Oh, wow.

E: Look, Chris. I realize, before we talk about anything else, we have to clear the air. I know what the CDH thing looks like. It looks like their CFO—me—must either have been a major crook or a major fool and patsy. I mention my title to most networkers and the color drains out of their face, like they just sat down with Al Capone or Typhoid Mary.

C: Well, the papers made it sound pretty bad, Elmo.

E: Well, it *was* bad, Chris. I can't blame people for being uncomfortable talking with me. It's perfectly fair for rational people to wonder what my role really was, and if I can't persuade them that my role was above board, then I don't deserve to be hired by anybody.

C: Of course, *I'd* never make unfair snap judgments like that . . . .

E: Chris, I couldn't blame you if you did. Often, the best way to handle someone who might be a risk is just to stay clear of him altogether. That's why I think it's fairest to bring the issue up at the beginning of the meeting and not blind-side you with it later, you know?

Anyway, my cause is helped somewhat by the fact that the president of CDH has confessed to the feds that I was set up, that their "deniability" would be best if they brought in someone who wasn't part of the conspiracy. They cooked the books, and then let their hired lamb get all self-righteous if someone suggested evildoing. Now that the president has confessed, the issue hasn't been whether I was a crook, but how I could be so stupid as not to know I was in the middle of a scam. Couple of days ago I got helped out on that score when the U.S. Attorney for the Southern District of New York said this was one of the smartest scams his investigators—all CPAs— had ever seen, and that *they* had studied the facts and figures for months without figuring out how it was done. Even they needed an insider to explain how they did the sleight-of-hand.

Now, I don't know if this makes you feel any more comfortable, Chris, but it makes me feel a lot more comfortable, because I need everyone to know that the subject is not taboo and that I'm comfortable talking about it.

Debrief

"Validating the aggressor" can be very useful when any factor in your profile or your past—your speech impediment, your wheelchair, the six months you spent in a hospital being treated for clinical depression—is so sensitive that people may not be comfortable asking about it and so significant that, if unresolved, it threatens your employability.

The key here is that *you* raise the issue, calmly and without defensiveness, signaling the contact that it's all right for him to talk about it. The suspicions of the "aggressor" generally are best imputed to unnamed third parties, rather than attributed to the person you're meeting with. That is, it works better not to say, "I bet you're wondering if my low-key personal style means I couldn't command respect from my staff." Most people will defensively deny having any such unsavory thoughts. Say instead, "In the course of networking around, I've run into several people who clearly have some concerns about my soft voice and low-key style. And that's fair. If I were in their shoes, I'd want assurance that my sales manager could exercise authority when necessary."

The "validating" part is essential. You must underscore that *it's OK* to harbor predictable suspicions and concerns—that any *fair* and *prudent* person might have the same concerns. After you validate, then you take on what trial lawyers call "the burden of persuasion." You offer, calmly and concisely, the information that shows why the aggressor's suspicions are in fact unfounded. The technique takes planning and practice, but it's an effective tool for getting skeletons out of the closet.

In the course of your networking, you're bound to encounter a number of other situations or glitches that require adroit handling or fast thinking. Some of these are described in the following sections.

Global Validation

When contacts are afraid they have no specific useful information, they'll often resort to blanket assurances ("With splendid credentials like yours, Myrna, you'll have absolutely no trouble finding a job") or global generalities ("In today's changing world marketplace, those who don't adapt will soon be as extinct as the dinosaur, so it's essential that you keep your mind open and your skills up to date").

When someone does this to you, first acknowledge and thank them for their "wisdom," then bring them gently back down to ground level, here and now:

> I really appreciate your viewpoint on my marketability, Rolf, because I think every job seeker worries about that. Now, in terms of specific activity I might

undertake to locate all those people who would find my credentials attractive, can you think of anyone in particular I might make a call to?

Conversing with the Ignorant

If yours is a highly technical or arcane field of employment, describing your strengths or objectives in jargon or shoptalk terms may befuddle a contact who isn't in your field and leave him totally unable to describe you to someone else. It may take considerable practice to learn to describe your desired position in comprehensible terms without being patronizing. In such situations, it's often easier to describe what you *do*—breaking your role into specific functions—than to use technical nomenclature to describe what you *are*.

An interesting drill, mentioned earlier, is to collar an eight-year-old and see whether you can communicate—enough for the child to paraphrase back to you— what you do:

> Nan, when a company wants to make a new medicine or drug—like your cough medicine—it can't simply make something up and go sell it at the drug store. First of all, there has to be a lot of research to see what chemicals will work and what ones won't. That takes a long time. Then they do a whole lot of carefully organized testing, first on rats and other animals and then, if things are going OK, on human beings. The government watches over this whole process very carefully to make sure that the new medicines actually work and that they don't accidentally have some bad side effects. There are a bunch of very detailed rules that have to be followed or else the drug can't be produced and sold. My job at Interalia Pharmaceuticals is to be in charge of that whole process of meeting government requirements during the stages from research through testing and then producing and selling. I'm responsible for doing this—it's called "compliance"—for over 50 drugs. Some are already on sale, some are being tested, and some are just being invented. It is very complicated work that requires me to pay a lot of attention to detail, but I've been doing it a long time, and I really like it.

Options for Change

Career shifters often have difficulty conveying a clear sense of focus because their skills and abilities might work well in a variety of roles or settings. When a contact asks, "What do you want to do next?" it can be hard to suggest the breadth of options without sounding unfocused. Most people can comfortably remember three general categories, particularly if you describe them starting with the most specific and concrete and moving to the more abstract:

> There are a couple of directions I want to explore, Norma. *Perhaps most logical* would be a position quite similar to what I've been doing—performing evaluations and analyses of companies for investment purposes. A similar analysis would take place when a company is being evaluated as an acquisition candidate by an investment banker, so it wouldn't be much of a stretch to make that switch. *Several people who know me also have suggested* that I should look into venture capital. It too requires good business judgment and evaluation ability, and might actually be a better fit with my strong sense of autonomy and willingness to take risks. *Finally, I've been looking into* something relatively different: developing a business that provides specialized training programs for CPAs, investment bankers and other financial managers. Here, my technical expertise in finance would simply be the basis for the business and not the business itself.

The Out-of-Sequence Meeting

Occasionally, a contact will have an agenda in mind for the meeting that differs markedly from your planning or expectations: "Sit down, Mary, and grab your pencil. I'll get my Rolodex out and let's run through some names." When the meeting deviates from the Exposure-to-Information-to-Names sequence most common in networking meetings, you can't very well yell, "Stop! You're doing this wrong! We have to do it my way!"

First, complete the activity at hand, whether you're jotting down names, reviewing the state of the world economy, or admiring the contact's prize goldfish. What you need then is a gentle but firm hand in circling the meeting back to the other agenda items:

> Bill, I appreciate your giving me all these referrals; several of them look like they'll be absolutely invaluable. Before we close, however, I did want to make sure I had explained clearly to you what I've been doing and what I want to do next, and I also had a couple of questions—other than asking for names—that I wanted to touch on with you briefly. Shouldn't take more than a few more minutes.

The Debunkers

You can expect to have a number of meetings in which the contact's sole agenda apparently will be to ridicule the networking process. If you reply by defending the process and sticking to your planned agenda, you may only fuel the flames. Instead, in a move like a tae kwon do maneuver, use the person's momentum to take him in the direction you want to go. Agree with him; take shots at the "networking" label; appear to be on his side:

> Boy, I'll say. I get it too, Ed. All these helpless people who ask for "a brief networking meeting" or "just 20 minutes" and come in with a little canned script. Doesn't it just drive you nuts? It's like they got themselves a little touchy-feely religion and everyone wants to self-actualize. Well, I never hired people to self-actualize on *my* front lawn, and I'll bet you don't either, Ed. I sure hope you don't think that's what I had in mind when I called. Actually, all I've been trying to do is get together briefly with some realistic business experts whose judgment I respect—like you, Ed—and bounce a few ideas off 'em. None of this "networking" garbage.

As we noted in the Introduction, there's no magic to the word "networking." You can spindle, fold, mutilate and lambaste the term without reducing the process's underlying strengths and utility. What matters is that there be effective meetings in which the parties are comfortable with the three main purposes that underlie networking's power: getting information, visibility and the names of others to whom the process can be extended. The point in networking isn't to ennoble the process; it's to learn to *use* the process.

"While you were out . . ."

8

Looping Back and Following Up

Congratulations! The meeting's over, you made it through alive, and you're "outta there." It went pretty well, don't you think? You were clear and succinct in your two-minute drill and your statement of your objectives. The Q&A provided some interesting insights, if no immediate leads, and the contact appeared eager to help. You closed the meeting strongly and promised to keep the contact posted on your progress. You've already made an appointment with one of the referrals he mentioned, and that fact is stated clearly in your thank-you note to him, which is in the mail.

You're done, right? All you have to do is repeat this process 120 more times and you'll have developed a spectacular network and succeeded in getting a lot of market exposure for yourself. Wait, though; there's more.

In Chapter 1, we compared each networking contact with an antenna. In your networking meetings, one of your main goals is to get each of these many antennae "tuned to your frequency" so that they'll be sensitized to listen for and retain information that might be of value to you. Even if they aren't able to help right now, they may overhear some gossip next week or next month that may turn out to be the key to your next job.

The problem is in harvesting all this information. You can't rely on every contact to call you each time he hears a juicy morsel that could be of use. If you've lodged the image of yourself firmly in his perceptual apparatus, he may think of you momentarily, file the data away somewhere in his head, and promptly forget about it the moment his mind turns to newer or more pressing matters.

If your contact learns of some really major news (like an incredible job opening that only he knows about), he might take the time to call. After all, the call could make him look really good and "prove" that he truly does know all there is to know. The potential for such a rich gratification may prompt him to take time out from his busy life and give you a ring.

But don't count on hearing from many of your contacts. They said they'd "keep their eyes and ears open" and get in touch if they "hear of anything interesting," but they were probably just being polite. All your antennae are out there, sucking up information, and not necessarily doing anything with it.

War Story: The seven-year itch

Our friend Calvin, the engineer-turned-lawyer whose two-minute drill was presented in Chapter 2, was busily networking among Philadelphia's venture capital community. Several people said he ought to meet Richard Bruton, but warned that Bruton was extremely hard to see. Calvin put it off until he had a spare moment one afternoon, and then placed an introductory call. Seconds after the secretary put him on hold to "see if Mr. Bruton is in," Bruton picked up and said, "Calvin, could you get over here right now?"

Ten minutes later, he was ushered into Bruton's office. "Glad to meet you, Calvin," said Bruton. "Do you know someone named Liam O'Brien?" Calvin searched his memory bank: "I remember him. He was my opponent in some oral arguments in my very first case ever at Bigg, Large & Humongous. This was about seven years ago. I was a rank beginner, and he carved me up something awful. I learned a lot that day."

Bruton smiled. "He's been my next-door neighbor for 20 years. He came over to my patio for a drink about seven years ago and said, 'Dick, I argued some motions this morning against a young lawyer who I think may be the smartest person I've ever seen. He is something out of the ordinary, with unbelievable maturity and business judgment for someone his age. If he ever crosses your path, you ought to take a hard look at him, make a job for him if you have to.' He has never said that about any other person in the years I've known him," said Bruton, "And, out of the blue, he brought you up again about four years ago: 'Did you ever run across that Calvin kid? Lord, he was impressive.' I really remembered that, Calvin."

"So now," Bruton continued, "it's seven years later, and out of the blue you call me. One glance at your resume and I knew it was you. Boy, I thought I'd never meet you. I know what goes around comes around, but that's really pushin' the envelope, don't you think? Anyway, might you be interested in doing some business with an old war-horse like me? I got some capital I need to stick somewhere, and if you can come up with some good ideas, I think you could count on some significant seed money."

This story is a reminder that what goes around does come around; we just can't predict when. Maybe it has already come around for you and you don't know it. Calvin reported having mixed emotions after his meeting with Bruton: on one hand, he'd struck networking gold; on the other, that gold had been available to him for years and he didn't know it. The possibility that there might be scores of similar untapped resources should be enough to drive Calvin—and every other networker—into a frenzy of follow-up activity, in addition to all the other tasks associated with the networking process.

The better your networking goes, the harder it will be to build systematic follow-up into your typical day. Say you expand your network to 100 contacts, and scheduling, calling, recalling and finally chatting with each of them requires ten minutes per follow-up. If you're following up every two months, then, during a six-month job search, you'll have to expend about 3,000 minutes (50 hours) on follow-up activity alone.

Few networkers are disciplined enough to build that kind of effort into their planning, particularly when it's more exciting to make new contacts than to cultivate existing ones. Besides, the vast majority of follow-ups won't have anything new or earth-shattering to tell. Following up isn't fun, but it's essential.

Keeping Your Image Fresh

Fortunately, effective follow-up doesn't require subjecting yourself and your contacts to more full networking meetings. Follow-up is done most efficiently by phone, and the call needn't take more than a couple of minutes—unless, of course, the contact has information to share or initiates a longer conversation.

Follow-up calls stand the best chance of getting through first thing in the business day or after 5:00 P.M. (the times when people are most likely to pick up their own phones). This fact argues for planning your follow-up activity as a daily ritual, another component of the structured daily process of reviewing and answering ads, reading newspapers and periodicals, doing library or database research, updating your master networking list (see Chapter 9), prioritizing possible new contacts, writing meeting request letters, making meeting request calls and keeping all your meeting appointments.

People who have a natural sales aptitude find this a natural approach to following up. They are perfectly comfortable calling and talking to strangers, and they look forward to reestablishing contact with people they've already met. For them, cold calling is routine and following up with some contacts daily is actually fun. Says one extrovert:

> Running a job search is simply selling a product, only you're the product. And don't tell me you're not a natural salesperson. If you're running a job search, you're in sales for the duration of the search, whether you like it or not. If you don't like it, then run a better search and make it end faster. Backing away from the tasks that every person in sales must master won't make the process more comfortable. It'll just make you feel guilty and keep you unemployed.

This common-sense advice notwithstanding, many of us approach the phone with dread, and the thought of following up for 30 or 45 minutes each day is

---

FOR YOUR INFORMATION

NATIONAL FOLLOW-UP DAY

Instead of building daily follow-up into their regimen, some networkers prefer to set aside a major chunk of time and just wade in. "It's like medicine," says one networker. "I can tolerate it far better if I take it in large doses, all at once." In this approach, a list of perhaps 30 names is selected for follow-up and prioritized. A day is set aside, and the networker sees how many can be reached before terminal boredom sets in.

This approach is better than no follow-up at all, but it has its disadvantages. It will require calling at least some contacts during times in the business day when they're least likely to be available, and it can be hard to remain fresh and upbeat. Your inquiries may sound flat and automatic after the 10th or 15th call.

unpalatable. "I feel like such a nag," says Margaret, a compensation and bene-fits specialist. "It's so transparent. It's like I'm calling to say, 'You didn't help me enough in the networking meeting, so can you do more for me now?"

Whether you make your follow-up calls once a week or once a year, you can take the edge off of the call if you start by giving help rather than asking for addi-tional assistance. As you make your daily rounds, you too are gathering anecdotal information. In fact, because your networking involves systematically trafficking in information, you're probably more attuned to stray bits of gossip than the aver-age person. A high percentage of the tidbits you hear will make you think of some-one you've networked with. File that information somewhere, and use it as your opener when you make a follow-up call.

Suppose, for example, you're networking in real-estate facilities management:

> Jill, I heard a piece of information yesterday that made me think of you. Did you know that All-States building management had a big fight with your competi-tor, Custodial Services Inc., and jerked their contract? That means that right now All-States has 58 office buildings under management—I looked it up—without any way of getting them cleaned. You may want to give them a call.
>
> While I have you, I also wanted to let you know that Shannon McCulloch was a really super lead, but that Barney James is no longer with DynamiCon. I've not been able to track him down. Have you heard where he might have gone? In any event, you may want to mark your Rolodex.
>
> I've got several things cooking at the first-interview stage, but nothing that I think will ripen into the job of my dreams. When we talked, you men-tioned some building maintenance companies in northern Illinois that you have a supply-buying co-op with. Have any of them mentioned a developer or client in their area that might need management or leasing help?

Frankly, it's not important whether Jill has already heard the information about her competitor or not. If she hasn't, you're providing her with real value, and the Rule of Reciprocal Favors ("I'll scratch your back; you scratch mine") comes into effect. She owes you one. If she has already heard the news, you still develop good-will simply by showing that you're thinking of her, are attuned to her interests, and will take the time to call her when you hear interesting gossip.

This technique of using information as your ice-breaker determines the pri-ority of whom you call for follow-up. You have to call contacts while the informa-tion is still fresh ("Did you hear, the *Titanic* sank?" won't earn you many points), so part of your structured follow-up planning should be set aside for "current events calls."

In this same vein, you can take steps that have no immediate follow-up value but can pay huge dividends later on. Foremost among these is sending your con-tacts articles, press releases, periodicals or research information of interest to them. This tactic works best if you don't explicitly (or implicitly) request immediate help in return. Just clip out or copy the article and stick a note-tag on the front: "Don, this reminded me of our conversation about widgets. Thought you might find it interesting. Best, Dick Jones." Any business referral you can make to a contact will earn you considerable goodwill, even if it doesn't pan out. Everyone responds warmly to the idea that someone has their economic interests at heart.

Structuring the Follow-Up Call

When it comes time to make follow-up telephone calls, you should at least have thought through the agenda for each call so that you don't meander aimlessly after connecting. Some reality checking is an essential part of this agenda. Just because you vividly remember your meeting with the contact doesn't mean that he recalls the meeting, you, what was discussed or what he may have promised to do. You may have to quickly and adroitly refresh his memory. Here are some sample scripts for various follow-up purposes.

Identity Reality Check

Bill, this is Amos Smith calling. You may remember that we chatted a couple of months ago at the suggestion of Noel Kissinger. I was the one who had just resigned from United Food and Beverage.

(Don't force people into yes–no questions such as: "Do you remember me?" If they don't, they'll either feel awkward or have to lie.)

Status Reality Check

When we spoke, I was concentrating my job search on product development roles with snack-food manufacturers in the Southeast. That's still my main focus, although I've expanded my search to the West Coast. Some friends have also suggested that my background would translate readily into new product development in other consumer products, so I've begun to look into that area, as well.

Refresher on Meeting Content

When we met, you gave me a lot of information about RJR Nabisco and told me about the competitor analysis your market research company had just completed on snack foods. You may remember that I mentioned a couple of Southern companies that hadn't been surveyed, and we also wondered about where Barney Jones had moved to.

Summary of Your Progress

Since we met, I've contacted 20 or so people, and everything suggests that there may be a better market in Southern California than here on the East Coast. Several people echoed your thought that I may need formalized marketing training if I want to get out of product design, and I've signed up for an intensive consumer product marketing course at State U. In general, my years with Yum-Yum Foods seem to be well received, but there has been some curiosity about why I left there to go to United. So, as you suggested, I've spent some time making sure my tale makes sense. By the way, Barney Jones lives in Brazil now.

Reenlistment of Help and Gentle Recall of Past Promises

I was calling this morning to see if you've heard of any leads or gossip I ought to be following up. You indicated that you were going to the national consumer products marketing convention, and said that you'd mention my availability to a couple of guys you used to work with. I was just wondering if you had a chance to talk with those guys and, if so, what my next step should be.

Closing and Agreement on Future Contact

Again, Bill, I really appreciate your help, and I'm grateful for your willingness to mention me to your colleagues. I hope I'm not making a pest of myself, but your advice and perspective have clearly been the most useful, from among all the people I've talked with. I'll certainly keep you posted on where things go from here. Would there be any problem if I looped back with you by phone, say, toward the end of the month?

Next Steps

Thank-you notes for telephone follow-ups probably aren't necessary (and would be a logistical nightmare), unless someone has provided you with a piece of information that calls for immediate action on your part. If that information leads to something solid and promising, feedback to the contact is in order. Even here, however, the phone is probably an easier and more effective medium. The exception would be if the new information actually gets you a job offer. A note announcing your success is the best way to cement what now will be a continuing relationship of a different sort.

Unfortunately, the majority of follow-up calls aren't going to produce valuable new information or insights. They'll only succeed in reenergizing your antennae and making sure they're still tuned to your frequency. But you'll be gratified to see how often a follow-up call proves timely and serves to jog the contact's short-term memory:

Judith! Good to hear from you! What a coincidence! I was thinking of you the other day. They just announced that the National Institute for Health is going to fund a pilot project to investigate how to do nationwide tracking of new tuberculosis cases in young adults. If the pilot project works out, they want to make it into a permanent program with a staff of perhaps ten, all across the country. I thought of you right away. With your background in public health and your new degree in computer science, it would be a natural for you. And I know the person you should call . . . .

You can look at the frustrations and rewards of following up in one of two ways: (1) You can rail against the outrageous inefficiency of a process that has you spending countless hours that appear to produce little or (2) you can live for those moments when the probabilities go your way and a follow-up call produces an unexpected boost to your fortunes.

Whether you love follow-up, tolerate it, or just plain hate it, it's an essential step in taking over and maintaining control of your future career.

FOR YOUR INFORMATION

BEWARE THE DREADED OVERKILL

One networker took our command to follow-up seriously and began to loop back with one particular contact at regular intervals. The intervals were weekly, Wednesdays at 3 P.M., like clockwork. He was polite and considerate but a little passive ("What can you do for me?"), and he didn't force conversations to run too long. But in about the fourth week, the contact blew up: "Listen, Mario. I haven't signed up to be your personal career consultant. You're a nice guy, but you're really abusing my time and my patience. I hope your search goes well, but I've given you all the help I'm going to give you. I'm sorry, but your regular Wednesday calls are no longer welcome."

The life of a networker is a lonely one, and it feels good when someone takes an interest in you and offers continuing support. But this isn't a friendship yet; it's only a cordial relationship created to serve a particular end: your career development. The success of networking in general is a triumph of "the strength in weak ties." But remember, they are *weak* ties! Be careful not to lean on these fragile relationships too hard.

How Often, Then?

During the job search, every one of your contacts should hear from you in some way, shape or form every two or (maximum) three months. A lot goes on in three months; the job market, the national economy, the state of the world all can assume an entirely new face within 12 weeks. If you check in every six months (and let's hope you're not in the job market that long), you're like a reemerging hermit. People will ask whatever happened to you. They'll say they assumed you'd found work. Out of sight, out of mind. Rusty antennas, no news.

Some networking job hunters have forsaken the direct time demands of personally following up in favor of writing and mailing newsletters, "action updates" or even printed brochures. This technique shares the merits and demerits of all direct-mail efforts: your exposure is maximized, but the likelihood of response is reduced.

A mailing of this sort—particularly if done artfully or with a little humor—can generate some interest, but it can't create the same obligation to help you that a personal conversation will. Therefore, although such "broadcast" mailings may generate momentary interest in your situation and greatly enhance your exposure, they too must be followed up with a personal phone call. The cost–benefit analysis of such efforts, therefore, turns largely on how unique or attractive your skills are, how broad a geographical spread you're trying to reach and how much time you want to spend on the telephone.

FOR YOUR INFORMATION

PRIORITIZE YOUR FOLLOW-UP

When planning the most logical way to prioritize your follow-up activity, consider this sequence:

1. Contacts who have made you promises, have demonstrated an active interest in helping you or have suggested specific time frames for looping back to them.
2. Proximity contacts—friends, relatives and colleagues who should be kept informed of your progress.
3. Perspective contacts—those most apt to be in the information flow and therefore sources of current information, if not active intervention, on your behalf.
4. Power contacts—people of whom you can ask one or two specific favors, but who have no reason to dedicate their lives to your well-being.
5. Distant contacts—those to whom you want to maximize market exposure but minimize the time allocated to be spent on them.

9

Planning, Logistics and Keeping Track

After you've invested two or more weeks in an energetic networking campaign, you'll find that your desk, purse, wallet, pockets and briefcase are overflowing with slips of paper. They will include cocktail napkins with apparently random phone numbers bleeding through the design, business cards with other phone numbers scribbled on the back, matchbooks covered with miniature hieroglyphics, 5 × 7 cards covered front and back with detailed notes and magazine reply cards on which are written the names of people you don't even remotely recognize.

These are the artifacts of aggressive networking, the "data dump" where all the information you've been collecting is first stashed. This is raw information:

untabulated, disorganized, often undated or unattributed. What separates systematic and effective networkers from bulls just crashing around in contacts' china shops is how these raw materials are processed and managed. Unless religiously controlled, integrated and planned, networking can produce too much information, not too little.

When this happens, many networkers, deluged with data and faced with far more to do than time to do it in, throw in the towel. They grab for the latest or most promising information and let the rest drift out of sight and out of mind. They forget to follow up (or forget whom they were supposed to follow up with). They may give themselves a "well-deserved" day of rest . . . or maybe two days . . . or a week. When they decide to regain momentum or try to regain control, they're confronted with all sorts of time-consuming tasks:

☆ Developing, integrating, purging and updating the networking master list.

☆ Prioritizing contacts (A, B, C, D; proximity/perspective/power; phone vs. in-person).

☆ Making phone calls to schedule meetings; calling back on the phone calls that don't connect; keeping track of how often the calls have been made; writing request letters to the contacts who should be seen in person.

☆ Following up on networking request letters.

☆ Keeping an accurate calendar of meetings scheduled, "drop dead" dates for follow-up letters, conferences, lunches and conventions.

☆ Keeping a current tracking system that allows retrieval of information on the people seen, when they were seen, what was discussed in the meetings and what action steps come next.

☆ Maintaining a current list of networking names, addresses and phone numbers.

☆ Taking the time to summarize and synthesize all that has been learned as the job search has progressed: objectives; attractive target industries or organizations; people and personalities.

For many networkers, the confrontation with all these administrative tasks is followed by what computer types call a "head crash." The whole system shuts down, circuits take themselves off-line, and an overwhelming urge develops to watch the afternoon ball game on TV. This denial response usually is accompanied by a pervasive sense of guilt and the horrible fear that other people out there aren't goofing off and are therefore building a competitive advantage in the job market.

Recognizing and Resisting the Rescue Fantasy

A common psychological response to such stress is what might be called the "rescue fantasy": a sense (often tinged with a slight euphoria) that there's no point in putting all sorts of systems and procedures in place when you aren't going to be in the job market long anyway. Your neighbor has confided, "I know some folks who will be real interested in you." The headhunter has said, "Your credentials are very impressive, very marketable." Perhaps the last time you ran a job search, your very first interview produced a good fit. Perhaps you feel that you're so qualified in your field that the world of work will seek you out.

This rescue fantasy results in a tendency toward passivity, even among people who long have been high achievers, active performers and strong self-starters. Don't confuse this tendency with laziness. Indeed, people acting out a rescue fantasy may show an unusually high energy level, but their energy isn't being directed toward structured, controlled job search behavior. Often, job seekers mired in this kind of approach–avoidance behavior report moving restlessly or compulsively from one task to the next—mowing the lawn, taking the car in for new brakes, cleaning up the study "so I can really get going on this job search thing," fixing the screen door, and so on. Typically, this activity is purposeful and has some utility: "Geez, Gladys, it's not like I'm sitting home watching daytime TV or something."

The Tie between Temperament and Purpose

The tendency to confuse motion with action may be even more marked among those who have little natural inclination toward detail-oriented or repetitive activity. According to the Myer–Briggs Type Indicator (MBTI), by nature about 60 percent of us (called "S-types" in MBTI jargon) are fairly comfortable dealing with detail, marshaling and organizing facts and plugging along with repetitive chores until a task is done.

Many others, however, find dealing with detail particularly frustrating. These "N-types" prefer to look at the big picture, devising strategies and leaving their implementation to others. They understand the crucial importance of details, but they are far more comfortable dealing with concepts and abstractions. They want to know "the most efficient approach to getting this job search over," and they hate it when they're told: "There's no such thing as an efficient job search, because the job market is inherently disorganized. The best you can hope for is an effective job search, which means trying everything, running down every detail and plugging along until the right job is found."

As a general proposition, S-types run better job searches than N-types do; they're more methodical, better organized, less impatient and less distressed when each and every networking meeting doesn't produce big hits or immediate results. Reminded that "what goes around comes around," the N-types retort, "How do I get it to go around faster?"

FOR YOUR INFORMATION

REALITY CHECK

The rescue fantasy and other job search stresses are symptoms of a broader syndrome: a sense of losing control. Reestablishing and maintaining control during a job search is a matter of giving equal attention to four factors:

1. Developing and conveying focus;
2. Developing and maintaining structure in your efforts;
3. Following up: Making sure the next step gets taken (or taking it yourself);
4. Maintaining a high activity level in all job search tasks.

So far we've emphasized the focus, follow-up and high activity themes. Now let's look at some ways of developing the most important element of control: structure.

Planning Forward, Tracking Back

Most job seekers tend to spend a lot more time organizing for what's to come than making sure they can retrieve information about what's already happened. How many of us, for example, crumple up telephone return-call slips and throw them away the moment we return the call? "There! That's done," our subconscious says. Later, we are on our hands and knees in front of the wastebasket, trying to find the slip that shows the name and number of the person offering the discount rate on floppy disks.

When networking, it's absolutely essential that you have systems in place, both to schedule future activity and to trace every single past call, letter or meeting. For most people, this means having a number of systems running in parallel:

1. A month-at-a-glance diary to give you a quick and global look at your future and past meeting activity.

2. A week-at-a-glance diary that shows your schedule of immediate meetings and provides a little space for an address, the referral's name and any other relevant notations regarding each contact.

3. A daily "to-do" form that charts first calls, call-backs, meetings, follow-up calls and other activity ticklers. (Prior days' lists should be kept chronologically, for historical purposes.)

4. A current Master Networking List, usually updated weekly, that records and prioritizes each contact. (Prior weeks' lists should be kept for historical purposes.)

5. A chronological Master Activity Summary (if not already included in the Master Networking List) that tracks, for each contact, the dates of (a) the initial referral; (b) the initial and all subsequent phone contacts, with a summary of the purpose and outcome of each; (c) a summary of the content of each meeting; and (d) the names of referrals obtained in each meeting.

6. A 5 × 7 card-catalog, Rolodex or computerized address list of every contact and referral. (This is best kept separate from your regular business Rolodex, and is useful if you want to reach a contact but don't want to wade through your Master Activity Summary chronologically just to find the phone number.) You may also use it to note "care and feeding" contacts for your existing network on a long-term basis: when you called, when you sent congratulatory letters, when you sent greeting or holiday cards.

Detail-oriented people who love structuring things say they get excited just looking at the list of all these control mechanisms. Their minds fly immediately to how they will format them, how long it will take to make daily entries, even what time of day will be set aside to keep the tracking/planning system current.

Concept-oriented people say the prospect of all this record keeping is daunting; a common rationalization is: "It looks like it may be more trouble than it's worth."

What you choose to do is a function of your temperament, your innate organizational abilities and/or your need for a sense of control. The record shows, however, that superbly organized and controlled searches tend to end faster and produce more choice than the throw-all-the-cocktail-napkins-and-matchbook-covers-into-an-accordion-file approach. The more sophisticated your systems, the more demanding they are of your time. Once set up, they won't update themselves.

Some networkers set aside one morning a week for updating and cleaning up their tracking/planning systems. The problem with this approach is that one missed week produces a deluge of data to process the next week. In the face of spending many hours making and updating entries, some job seekers let it slide. The magnificently planned systems are abandoned, the job search becomes a day-to-day, make-it-up-as-you-go-along affair, and valuable information disappears from the job seeker's grasp forever.

Whether you prefer manual tracking systems where you push paper or automated programs where you manipulate bits and bytes is pretty much a matter of personal preference and your level of computer literacy. Beyond the bulkiness of maintaining manual files, just knowing that the hard copy is forever retrievable may be comforting. Networkers who are adept on the PC find "working in paper" incredibly archaic. They report that it's fun to design their own database filing system, use one of the increasing number of user-friendly database software programs now commercially available, or take an existing system and adapt it for the demands of networking and job search planning.

If you're going to track activity manually, it makes sense to design and use a series of forms that promote uniformity in the way you elicit, structure and retrieve information. There's no particular magic to the layout of such forms, as long as they work for you. A weekly job search plan, while resembling a standard week-at-a-glance calendar, forces the job seeker to review and think of each of the many interrelated activities that go into a comprehensive job search. A condensed form can easily be scaled up. One job seeker who has a background in military project management created a continuous wall-chart timeline that now extends across two walls of his basement. It's his "life-at-a-glance."

Automated Structure

A trip to the local PC dealer or software vendor may either delight or bewilder a networker looking for organizational aids. The trade-off usually seems to be between user-friendly applications that can be learned quickly but don't allow much custom-tailoring, and highly sophisticated interactive database products that can be expanded, contracted, folded or pleated to present information in almost any form the user finds most practical.

Many bundled programs contain basic word-processing, spreadsheet, calendar and list generation functions in one package; in some programs, it's possible to move rapidly and easily from function to function: composing letters, doing merged mailings or updating lists. The downside of many of these simpler programs is that they require item-by-item information entry, and the information is presented only in a certain prescribed format. For more sophisticated computer jockeys, highly interactive databases can be developed that distinguish between summarizing past activity and tackling future tasks, such as generating daily "to-do" lists.

Figure 9.1 shows a sample page from the hard copy printout of the networking status report of "Charlie." Before commencing his job search, Charlie had been using a marketing database called Act One to develop a specialized medical service business. When the market for his services went soft and he chose to discontinue marketing efforts, he converted the system to serve as his networking planner, tracker, notepad and nag.

Charlie keeps his computer on 24 hours a day (computers don't mind that). When he sits down to make a phone call, he has the phone number, contact's name and history and next planned step visible in front of him. He chooses to use a headset for phone calls; people talking with him can hear the *click-click!* of keyboard strokes as he enters and updates relevant information. Immediately after getting back from meetings, Charlie tries to update the database while the information and next steps are fresh in his mind. If that's not possible, he allocates his

Figure 9.1   Networking Status Report

Notes and History for Date(s): 12/09/94–12/17/94

Rpt. Date: 12/17/94   Time: 12:44P

Name: Allied Capital Initiatives

PH: 215-647-8256 x: n/a

Contact: Melvin Dorrance

Status/ID: Prospect

Title: VP, Bus. Devel.

Referral: Edwin Jones III

Notes: 12/16/94: Position filled shortly after my resume received. Impressed with my credentials; has sent resume around company. May get a call from Alan Kipkae, VP Mktng, if interested.

History:	Type:
Description:	
12/17/94	ID/Status
Prospect	
12/16/94	Last Results
Job filled; sent resume to both VP Mktg	
12/16/94	Call
Attempt: 10:47 A. F/U: Resume faxed	
12/15/94	Call
Received: 10:47 A. F/U: Fax resume	
12/11/94	Call
Attempt: 1:55 P. Sec'y: Call next week	

Figure 9.2   Partial Contact List—Most Recent Activity

Status/Results/Next Steps Report

Page: 1   Report Date: 1/27/94   Time: 4:11P

No. of Profiles: 271

Company:

Contact:

Next Steps:

Festerbrand Co.
Joseph Mintz
Sent ltr; Call to f/u

Partners: Carter Siluvish
Sev poss w/portfolio co's. Will review w/partners

Adams Associates
Devon Adams
Nothing now; poss something late spring

AdvanceCare, Inc.
Ramona Fledge
Had n/w mtg; gave intro to Steve der Haalt

AFR/Tustin Venture Capital Fund
Casey Gregg
Call per David Vizier and use his name

Arthur Andersen & Co.
Stavros Bloehn
Mark Blanchard
Rufus Kahn
Will f/u w/clients & make referrals; chk back w/Bloehn

BDX Speidel
Robert Thanatogenos
Spoke on phone; ltr sent; call week of 1/18/95 to f/u

Blass, Suder & Rosenthal (attys)
Kevin O'Brien
call late in day, wk of 1/14/95 to sched mtg.

Beacon, Davitt & Nelson, CPA
Kendell Davitt, CPA
Disaster: confused me with someone else; rough phone call; no call back

first working hour each day to making his database current, answering ads or using the word processor to generate other correspondence.

Sophisticated databases can be reconfigured to add or delete "fields" (specific items of information). Charlie continues to fiddle with his Act One variations: after networking for a while, he found it useful to have the program print out only the last items of activity (Figure 9.2). His master file continues to log a complete chronological history of all activity. As shown in Figure 9.1, running a full printout, from A to Z, would consume a lot of paper.

You may want to experiment with a variety of approaches, discarding any that don't produce immediate practical benefits for you. Building the learning curve for mastering new computer applications may seem frustrating, especially if what you want most is to get "out there" and start networking. But in the long run, the servicing demands of a good system will enhance your self-discipline without making you feel like a slave to it. Charlie, for example, knows his system is demanding, but finds it a worthwhile source of structure and stability. If you ask Charlie how his networking is going, he'll tell you—and he'll tell you exactly:

> Some people say that I spend more time servicing the database than the value it provides is worth. True, it does require an absolute commitment to keep on top of data entry. But the fact is that I don't use this system because I'm a natural with computers (although I am) or because I'm a detail freak. I do it because, by nature, I'm terribly disorganized. Without this system to police me, I'd be lost. Yes, I spend a lot of time giving my policeman what it needs to police me, but, for me, it's more than worth it. Not only do I stay on top of what has become a very large database of names and activities, but when I put the system to use, I can do certain things very quickly. I don't have lots of binders and folders and indexes and cross-references. This system basically does it all.

10

Alternative Approaches and Techniques

Why is the most popular networking transaction a personal referral to someone, followed by a face-to-face meeting? Because it's easiest on everyone involved. It's by no means the only effective networking avenue, however, and it can be supplemented by a variety of other approaches and meeting styles.

As we noted earlier, modern networking owes much to executive search consultants (a.k.a. headhunters), who learned that personal contacts produce good information. Skilled and seasoned headhunters have legions of personal contacts they can call to get a search rolling. But they'll also tell you that a lack of an existing network or of a supply of personal referrals isn't an insurmountable barrier to commencing a smashing networking campaign. Cold calls work just fine, provided you become adroit at making a positive first impression on the phone, reducing the contact's defensiveness and getting to the point in a hurry.

Think of your own mental processes when your secretary says that someone whose name you don't recognize is on the line, or when you pick up the phone and hear an unfamiliar voice. Your mental organizing and risk-reduction apparatus immediately poses several frame-of-reference questions to which you want immediate answers:

1. Who are you?
2. Why are you calling me?
3. What do you want?
4. What are the stakes—upside and downside—in this transaction?

Every person you call cold will have the same issues and concerns, so be ready with the answers (even outline your opener if you have to):

> Mr. McKee, we haven't met, but I'd certainly like to meet with you. My name is Brent Anderson, and I'm calling to see if it might be possible to arrange a brief networking meeting at your convenience. I've read your articles on health care reimbursement policies, and I noticed that we both graduated from Kenyon College. I've just completed my Master's in Public Health at UCLA, and, before going back to school, I spent four years in emergency room operations at Cedars of Galilee hospital in Los Angeles. I now want to return to Chicago to continue my career, and everywhere I turn in the medical community around here, your name keeps coming up. Is there any chance we might get together?

Many networkers hate cold calls because they feel they're being intrusive and they're asking for an awful lot without the lubricant of a common acquaintance. All but the wildest extroverts among us tend to shy away from the prospect of calling a complete stranger and springing our personal agenda on them. In our mind's ear, the call sounds like this:

> Hi, you don't know me, but I'm running a job search and I would be desperately grateful if you'd meet with me and give me some of your precious time and advice and take responsibility for my life. You'll be risking personal embarrassment if I should turn out to be a complete turkey, but still should introduce me to all your friends and contacts.

FOR YOUR INFORMATION

TIPS FOR TELEPHONE NETWORKING

Getting a memorable message across while networking by telephone is harder than in person, but it is possible. The key to success in such calls lies in capturing and sustaining the contact's interest. Your tools for accomplishing this are limited. The contact can't appreciate your effortless grace, impeccable dress, warm smile, twinkling eyes, or affirming head-and-hand gestures. Without those supportive aids:

☆ Your agenda must be clearly focused and articulated.

☆ The content of your speech must be clear and concise.

☆ The delivery of your message must carry a lot of weight in building rapport, creating trust, establishing authority and sustaining interest.

Other than its increased focus and abbreviated duration, telephone networking parallels face-to-face networking by requiring: decompression, a brief self-description, a job search or career change objective, targeted Q&A, a request for names and referrals, a polite close and a promise to follow up.

Go ahead and feel that way; but your life and career are on the line. Compared with the assertive and insistent tone used by most headhunters, your call won't sound as presumptuous as you're afraid it will, and it's unlikely that you'll be treated like a telemarketing solicitor.

Identifying Your Granfalloons

In his book *Cat's Cradle,* Kurt Vonnegut, whose works embody a slightly out-of-control view of life that strikes a responsive chord with many networkers, invented an utterly spurious religion in which he introduced the notion of the granfalloon. A granfalloon is a group of people whose lives and fates appear somehow related, often by virtue of geographical happenstance, membership in some group or participation in a common activity.

In fact, there's no fundamental intersection between the interests and destiny of members of a granfalloon, but its members believe and act as if there is. Some typical granfalloons include:

☆ Hoosiers.

☆ The 1973 graduating class of Kansas State University.

☆ The United States Senate.

☆ Birdwatchers.

☆ All the others made sick by the driving of the tour bus driver on your most recent vacation.

☆ Every other General Counsel of a publicly held corporation.

☆ Aggies.

☆ Political button collectors.

☆ Unemployed job hunters over age 40.

Being a member of a granfalloon gives you some interpersonal leverage with other members. You can use that leverage to break the ice and establish a basis for asking for a little help:

> Jeff, I don't know if you remember me or not, but we were in the same graduating class at med school in '72. I've been getting in touch with a number of my old classmates to see if I might get a little advice and counsel as I work through a career shift . . . .
>
> ———
>
> Leah, this is Claude Bennett. Your daughter Deirdre and my son Ian go to the Fuzzy Bunny Day Care Center together. Listen, I'm in the middle of a job search, and I thought one way to get a little more market exposure would be to go through the center's parent directory, introduce myself to the parents of some of Ian's little friends, and maybe do a little informal networking . . . .
>
> ———
>
> Ed, this is Evan Monroe calling, from down in Tupelo. I've been calling a number of colleagues in the Business Forms Manufacturing Association to see if I might arrange to drop in on you when I make my rounds through Mobile early next month.

Granfalloons represent ready-made mini-networks that you can mine to broaden your market exposure without the greater discomfort of cold calling. You may be a member of scores of granfalloons, and each membership gives you a supply of people to whom you have a common bond (however minimal) and *whom you can call by their first names.* This last point isn't incidental to your comfort level. Adults—especially men—tend to dislike being forced into the superior–subordinate relationship implied by having to call someone Ms. or Mr. Last Name.

If you absolutely cannot think of any group of people with whom you have something in common, grab a directory—any directory—where you're already listed or could be listed if you wanted to pay a membership fee (and, if required, contribute to the goals of the organization you're joining). If you haven't checked out the astonishing variety of directories, databases and lists that are available today, you're in for a major surprise.

Compiling granfalloons is a real growth industry. You can even buy or rent granfalloons from direct-mail houses that compile mailing lists. Just tell one of these vendors the granfalloonian attribute you want to tap or the kind of person and position level you want to contact—officers, senior managers, researchers and so on—and they'll provide a list of current names for you to call or write. Want databases for academic, nonprofit or government sectors? They're all available. (Beware, though. Many of these databases are obsolete, incomplete and rife with errors. Ask to see a sample list, find out how frequently it's purged and updated, and then compare the pricing closely with competitors' charges.)

A few ground rules are in order when using granfalloons to extend your network:

1. Be sure to state the nature of your relationship at the beginning of your call. Don't let anyone wonder who you are and why you're using up valuable time.

2. Be clear that you're making contact with a lot of members of the granfalloon. To select one person and imply that you're asking him alone to help you is to suggest a level of duty that isn't supported by the facts.

3. State clearly the type and level of help you're asking for.

Here are some sample scripts:

At this point in my job search, Helene, I'm simply trying to contact as many Coolidge High grads as I can, to ask that they keep their ears attuned to any information about possible jobs for experienced programmers . . . .

―――

All I'm trying to do, Leo, is get the word out to as many Brothers of the Mystic Knights of the Sea as I can and ask that they think of me if they meet someone who needs a cracker-jack sales rep.

Because the level of help being requested in a granfalloon contact is so minimal, assume in the tone of your call that you're entitled to and will get that help. Don't water down your request with "if it's not too much trouble" or "if it's OK." The moment you assume the role of a supplicant, the power of a granfalloon's gentle peer pressure utterly vanishes. If in the name of finding a job, resuming your life and avoiding starvation you're not comfortable with this minimal degree of presumptuousness, then stay away from granfallooning.

When There Is No Place for Face-to-Face

We've emphasized the importance of networking in person whenever possible, both because people exchange a great deal of information nonverbally and because people remember faces better than they remember sound waves or written words. Sooner or later, however, your networking activity is going to lead you out of town, either because a valuable contact (or two) lives outside your one-day travel radius, or because, in your efforts to run a geographically diverse search, you are trying to develop "subnetworks" in far-off places.

FOR YOUR INFORMATION

WHY ARE YOU CALLING ME?

Even if you lack close personal connections for referrals, you can use other rationales to open doors, such as:

- ☆ I'm new to this town and I don't know anyone.
- ☆ I'm coming home after years of working overseas.
- ☆ I've read your book, and it transformed my life.
- ☆ Everyone says you're the leading expert around.
- ☆ I want to follow in your footsteps.
- ☆ We went to the same college or grad school.
- ☆ We have [something] in common.
- ☆ We're members of the same association or organization.
- ☆ We're peers in the same industry, even if we've never met.

When telephone networking, it's a good idea to outline your agenda in some detail before dialing. Have your self-introduction prepared and practiced (but not to the point of sounding canned and artificial). Have the general agenda and the specific sequence of issues you want to discuss written out in front of you. Understand that because a telephone networking conversation will be shorter than a personal meeting—40 minutes on the phone is an outrageously long time—you bear greater responsibility for steering the meeting, keeping it focused and making smooth and crisp transitions from one subject to the next.

Don't assume that you're immediately going to start networking when you first call. When you get to the point of describing what you want from the contact, you should offer the person the choice of proceeding now or scheduling a later, specific time to conduct the conversation:

> If it's not possible to get together for a brief meeting, I was hoping I might still get your advice and counsel for a few minutes on the phone. I realize that you weren't expecting my call, and I don't want to disrupt your busy schedule. If you have a few minutes now, that would be great; but if it makes more sense to arrange a time for me to call back, that's certainly fine, too. I have three or four areas I'd welcome your thoughts on, and I think we could cover all the bases in less than 15 minutes. If we would be less rushed at some other time, perhaps first thing one morning or at the end of a workday, I'll be happy to schedule a time to call back.

If the contact agrees to schedule a time, you absolutely must call precisely at that agreed-on hour! (Check for any difference in time zone.) If you're even five minutes late, you're likely to be dogmeat. Expect people to be even more protective of their time on the phone than they are of their time spent in personal meetings. Incoming calls may be income-producing calls for them, and they will not want their phone to signal "busy" to their clients.

During the call, listen carefully for any indication that the contact doesn't understand you, has missed the point or is irritated at something. Given the time constraints of telephone networking, there's an understandable tendency to speak rapidly and cram in as much information sharing as possible. Resist this temptation; if anything, slow your delivery down and finish your thoughts and sentences firmly. Run-on mouths suggest run-on minds, and you can't expect the same tolerance of hemming and hawing that you might get in a face-to-face meeting.

Be sure to conduct frequent reality tests: "Have I answered your question?" "Would it help if I elaborated on that a bit?" "Am I being clear?"

You won't gain the interest of contacts unless you sound truly interested in what you're trying to do. This isn't a telephone survey you're conducting; it's your only opportunity to convey a clear and attractive sense of your goals and attributes to someone you may never meet in person. Be animated without being hyper; be enthusiastic without sounding like a cheerleader or a pollyanna.

The best way to be engaging is to be engaged in the conversation. *Don't let your mind wander!* If you start playing with the cat, looking at the dust balls under your desk and saying, "Uh huh, uh huh, uh huh" over and over instead of concentrating on the conversation, the person on the other end of the line will know you're only going through the motions. The minute that happens, you can kiss rapport goodbye.

Long-Distance Networking

Long-distance job searches may require some long-distance networking. The reality of both is that you can't hope to canvass the entire country. You'll have to set some geographic priorities, then target only those areas. Your targeting may include planning a trip to a distant city and orchestrating a concentrated networking blitz while you're there. The key action is scheduling your first round of networking meetings before you arrive:

> Jerry, I got your name from Allan Kahn, who has told me a good bit about how you moved out to Spokane from New York. Listen, my spouse is being transferred to Spokane and we'll be relocating there early next year. I'm coming out for a brief reconnaissance visit in August, to check out the housing situation and to see whether I can do a little networking. I'm a CPA specializing in small and family-owned businesses, and I need to try to establish a beachhead for a new practice. Is there any chance we can get together on either August 14th or 15th? I'm sorry to box you in so tight, but that's the only time I can get out to meet my contacts. I'm not asking you to lead me to new clients, but I sure could use some help in just getting oriented. I'd really appreciate it if you could squeeze me in.

A good rule of thumb, if you can afford the motel costs, is to extend your trip to twice as many days as you've scheduled for your first round of networking meetings. If you've got one full week filled with 12 to 15 meetings, that's great! Leave a second week open to try to schedule an equal number of second-tier meetings stemming from your first-week's referrals. Find a local word-processing service before you go, or take along your laptop computer, portable printer, and some stationery. It may be essential to get out some quick thank-you notes or meeting request letters (which you'll hand-deliver). Set your motel room up like a command bunker, and attack the local networking scene for all you're worth.

Be warned: The two weeks will be exhausting. Your plight will elicit the sympathy of most contacts, however, and they'll be flattered that you're abandoning whatever place you live in now to join them in their fair city. Play to the hilt your sense of community and your desire to fit into this new setting. Before your trip, contact the local chamber of commerce and get a packet of information materials. Study it. The people you meet will be pleased and more helpful if they see you've done your homework before imposing yourself on them.

When you get back, use the initial contacts you generated to follow up by phone with people you met and to do some additional telephone networking. The fact that you've been out there and learned the lay of the land will allow you to focus on these calls and display your knowledge. People will warm to you, even if they can't see you face-to-face.

The Granfalloon Letter: Networking by mail

If you're running a geographically diverse job search and haven't focused on one or two cities in which to target a drop-in, *banzai* networking campaign, there's one quasi-networking technique that you can try. If you're prepared to sacrifice two of the three main benefits of networking—the reciprocal exchange of information and the acquisition of more names—you can get yourself an enormous amount of visibility by flooding the country with granfalloon letters rather than granfalloon phone calls. This technique is akin to saturation bombing: low efficiency, but potentially high effectiveness.

If you want to penetrate assorted granfalloons by mail, you should understand some rules of the game. Conventional job search wisdom says that mass mailings are low-probability vehicles. Perhaps no more than 5 percent of all jobs are located and landed through form letters sent out en masse. To make the most of this technique, moreover, you're supposed to follow up, with a phone call, each letter you send. Most mass mailings are a direct appeal for employment:

Dear Mr. Smith:

If your company should have or anticipate an opening for an experienced cost estimator, I would welcome your consideration. I'm highly motivated, dedicated . . . .

A granfalloon mailing takes an entirely different tack. It isn't a request for employment; it's a candid admission that you're simply looking for market exposure. In a traditional mailing, the stakes are high: "Please hire me and pay me a lot of your money." In a granfalloon mailing, the stakes are kept very low: "Please take note of who I am and what I do in case you hear of anyone who might need someone like me."

Because granfalloonian bonds are so thin, you can't ask for a lot of help without hopelessly overtaxing the relationship. Your request should be kept low-key and thrown casually into the topic sentence of your letter:

> I recently left my position as a chief process control manager at Zebcore Chemicals, and I've been writing to a number of colleagues to acquaint them with my credentials and ask that they keep me in mind if they hear of an appropriate opening . . . .

> ———

> Although we haven't met, I've never met another nuclear power plant control room engineer with whom I didn't have a lot in common. Which is why I'm writing to every senior-level engineer I can, to develop an informal network of colleagues as I run my job search . . . .

A granfalloon letter is a useful way to contact people who are your peers but may blow off your networking requests because they think you represent a threat to them. Many networkers report that they're shortchanged by potentially useful contacts because they represent some irrational danger to the contact's job security. This problem diminishes when you emphasize that you're a peer, not a competitor. The granfalloon letter can be adroitly cast to suggest an absolutely riskless agenda:

> Michael Trapp, Senior Vice President
> First Durango National Bank
> Durango, CO
>
> Dear Mike:
>
> During my 15 years as a Senior Vice President for Commercial Lending with Minnesota National Grain Bank, I periodically would get calls from recruiters looking for qualified candidates for senior-level banking management positions. Given your position and your seniority, I'd be surprised if you don't also get calls like this. That's why I'm writing.
>
> In a tight job market, all the experts recommend getting as much exposure as possible. To this end, I've been writing a number of banking executives like yourself, not to request that they hire me, but just to ask a simple favor. If you are contacted by a headhunter, I'd be grateful if you'd mention my availability (my job at MNGB was eliminated, along with 300 others, in May) and perhaps suggest where I can be reached.

Please understand, Mike, that I'm not asking for a reference; that would be presumptuous. But if I can simply get my name in play, I can champion my own cause from there. I've enclosed a copy of my resume, just to give you a feel for my background and experience. If you'd like any more information for any reason, I'd be delighted to chat with you. Meanwhile, thanks for your help. I certainly hope I can return an appropriate favor in the future.

Letters like this may produce no more than their stated purpose: a couple of calls from headhunters. But they also may find their way into a number of hands in the addressee's company and result in a request to "come out and chat. We might have something here for someone like you."

Understand that granfalloon letters are extremely low-efficiency items. You don't try to follow them all up personally—especially if you've sent out 400 or more. If this technique works at all, it's because of sheer volume. As one sage put it, "It's like standing on your back porch in the dark of the moon, firing your shotgun into the night. If you're willing to use up enough shells, you'll eventually get yourself a rabbit."

The Outer Limits: Other offbeat forms of market exposure

If your networking goal is solely to maximize exposure, there are other forms of outreach you may consider. All are inefficient and some are costly, but they may include one that turns the trick for you.

Some job seekers invite their network to spectate actively as the job seeker works through the adventure of changing employers by sending out what are, in effect, newsletters. These may look like personalized letters, or they may be styled as memos or press releases entitled "Action Update!" They may be postcards; a memorable one was a mailing of picture postcards depicting a glorious Tahitian sunset. The message on the back read: "Nope. I'm not here. I'm still in your city, trying every technique I can to find a new position as an ad agency creative director." Another creative type developed and mailed an elaborate four-color brochure and sent it out as a mailing to 250 creative types (at a total cost of $1.70 per mailing). All it said was, "Michael Stern, Graphic Artist." This was extraordinarily costly exposure, but its originality, quality and sheer daring got Michael a job.

There are several problems with any attempts to keep everyone in your network informed through mailings:

1. They're expensive, both in bucks and in the time and effort needed to prepare them.
2. They either require follow-up or they operate on the theory that if someone hears of something really hot, he'll call you.
3. If the job search extends a long time, the periodic updates become testimonials to your pain, your struggle or your ineffectiveness as a job seeker. They may then have the ironic effect of driving people away from a "drowning man" rather than encouraging support and help.

Formalizing the Network: Your own
advisory board

Many businesses and organizations have boards of directors or trustees to lend their collective judgment, evaluate progress, provide feedback, set operational priorities and plan the organization's activities. Some enterprising networkers have used this model to enlist the help of a group of acquaintances or colleagues to serve as a semiformal advisory board for their job search efforts.

These can't be casual acquaintances. They should be people who believe in you and are willing to invest considerable time and effort in your future. You're going to be asking a lot of them, and they should know this before committing to serve.

Perhaps once a month or every six weeks, your group should get together with you (you buy the beer and pizza) and systematically review your progress and plans. In order to work well and not become a cheerleading squad, your advisory board must agree to be disciplined, candid, realistic and, if need be, tough on you.

Before you ask five or six people to serve on your board for the duration of your job search, you must prepare some guidelines for their responsibilities: a mission statement, an outline of tasks and functions, and a description of their specific roles or expertise and the scope of their control. For each meeting, you must prepare an agenda and a status update report (including a statistical summary of ads answered, letters mailed, calls made, meetings held, follow-ups completed and so on).

For many networkers, the idea of a "continuing executive network" is too extreme, too formal, too demanding on the helpers, too time-consuming and too structured. For others, the idea of having a sustained source of objective feedback promotes a strong sense of stability and continuity in the job search. In networking, as in many other challenges of life, you must find approaches that feel good to you, that keep you energized or that convince you that you're capitalizing on opportunities that less adventuresome souls will never discover.

If you feel an approach or technique isn't working for you—if it's too uncomfortable or if its potential payoff is poor or speculative—abandon it. There are plenty of other approaches to occupy your time.

11

What the Future Holds

Most of us enjoy doing most what we do best. Conversely, there's a natural tendency to dislike activities that we haven't mastered and that make us feel awkward. For that reason, some networkers, after embarking on their first few meetings, will firmly believe that networking is the pits.

Not recognizing that they must walk before they can run, these try-outs translate their initial discomfort into a decision to bag networking and use other avenues to pursue their job search. They're making a big mistake.

Rather than giving up, think of a sports activity you tried to learn. Remember how you had fun even when you were on the early part of the learning curve?

The difference was that when you were learning tennis, a computer program or how to ride a horse, you probably were not being judged on the quality of your early efforts (and the stakes weren't terribly high). When networking, you're holding yourself up to others' scrutiny, and you're definitely being judged. The stakes in any particular meeting are low, but the whole purpose of networking is pretty serious: to find appropriate and meaningful employment and redirect your entire life.

No wonder, then, that the initial frustrations of networking (or the occasional major disappointment when a meeting goes horribly) turn off many networkers. They never get good enough to reap its benefits; they choose not to go around, so nothing comes around. Their resulting verdict is that networking doesn't work.

If you're lucky, your early meetings will include one in which someone is so supportive, or you learn so much or you get turned on to so many other people, that your adrenalin surges and boosts you through the initial insecurities and doldrums.

War Story: Light dawns on marblehead

This isn't as much a war story as it is a recurring event: it has happened numerous times in pretty much the same way. The career counselor has schooled a job seeker in basic networking technique, thrown him out bodily into the cruel world of networking, and seen him return from the first few meetings depressed, bummed out or convinced that he's a hopeless failure.

After about the fifth or sixth meeting, however, the counselor looks up and finds the job seeker leaning against the jam of his office door. The job seeker says, smiling a kind of wry grin:

> I'm not quite sure how to explain this, but I got into the meeting—nervous as usual—and sort of crashed my way through the decompression and launched into my two-minute drill.
>
> About halfway through, a peculiar realization came over me: *This Stuff is True.* I'm not making it up, I'm not embellishing it, I'm not trying to fool anyone. I'm only saying what's true. That means I can't possibly forget it, and I don't have to worry about losing my place in some script, because if I slip a cog, all I have to do is go back and tell the truth.
>
> Suddenly, I felt calm. I don't have to be a performer; I just have to try hard to be clear and get to the point. The meeting turned out to be really enjoyable. When I loosened up, the contact loosened up. I think we're on our way.

One of the strongest incentives to maintain your pace during your early efforts at networking is the enormous amount of energy you've already invested in your self-assessment and in developing your master contacts list and setting up a planning/tracking system. The prospect of seeing all that effort go to waste should motivate you. If it doesn't, the thought that countless other job seekers— many of them your competitors—are using the networking technique successfully should serve as propellant.

The first five meetings are hell (if they're not, then you're not extending yourself), but after you groove your swing and begin to control the process (rather than be controlled by it), momentum will develop naturally. This early, rocky period will also serve as a helpful model for weathering later stretches when things go momentarily flat in your search. The message for early-stage networkers, therefore, is to keep the faith and keep moving.

Maintaining Momentum When Things Bog Down or Blow Up

Once a job search is well under way, it's far more common for networkers to report that they have too much to do rather than too little. All those tasks—scheduling, tracking, planning, calling, meeting, following up—will keep you very busy. But there still may be times when the process slows or when you run low on new contacts or new directions.

Several factors can be at play here: It's not uncommon to have a harder time scheduling meetings during the summer, when more people are off on vacation. Candidates who conduct their searches within tightly defined geographical areas may find that they've succeeded in reaching the "major players": the high-profile prospective contacts in their area. But then they feel that there's no one new to meet. During recessions, the streets may be awash with legions of similarly credentialed job seekers, all trying to network with the same base of contacts—who, after a while, get tapped out, overused and fed up.

A good technique for sustaining momentum during a flat period is to change activities. If new meetings are proving hard to schedule, grab your tracking list and spend more time looping back and following up than you normally would. Go to the library and peruse the latest batch of directories to see whether you can identify some new granfalloons. Attend more conferences, meetings and luncheons—any gatherings where groups of people congregate—and you have an excuse to meet new contacts. Revise and update your tracking system; purge stale or useless information from your database.

Sometimes, a loss of momentum won't come from structural difficulties with the networking process itself, but rather from a transitory fit of the psychological blahs. We can talk forever about networking meetings being low-key, but the fact remains that they're often stressful. For natural extroverts and sales types, the pressure may not be felt keenly. But for many job hunters, having to constantly push forward to schedule, track, write, talk and explain themselves gets wearing after a while.

For those in desperate need of work or those whose natural tendency is to exercise fierce control over their lives, there may be a tendency to run a job search like a 100-yard dash rather than a paced, 10,000-meter race. Athletes who engage in endurance sports learn to keep just within their "aerobic threshold"—that is, to hold a pace where they can still breathe and not go into oxygen debt. If they exceed that threshold, they soon erode their physical and emotional resources. At that point, every problem looks twice as tough and every disappointment feels twice as keen. The same holds true with the rigors of networking and running a job search.

During your job campaign, be good to yourself. You may find that you need more sleep than when you were beating your brains out in your old job. Surprised? Don't be. This is new territory, and newness is stressful for all of us. You may gain (or lose) some weight. Unless this becomes so extreme that you look like either you have no self-control (and your clothes don't fit) or you've contracted some wasting disease, don't become preoccupied with a few pounds either way. First things first: find a great new job, then turn your focus to getting back into shape.

Do mind your health, however. Take an exaggerated approach to eating well and getting regular exercise. If you hate Brussels sprouts and jogging, you can delete them from your regimen after you start your new job. Have checkups twice as often as normal during a job search. See your dentist more often, too (changes in body chemistry caused by long-term stress can rapidly increase plaque formation).

Taking Time Out

If you utterly lose it and can't stand the prospect of one more meeting or another handwritten thank-you note, give yourself a vacation. Note, please, that we're not encouraging you to give in to the rescue fantasy: a nap here, a nod there, followed by six months of daytime TV. But schedule some time away from the job search—time that's solely for you and your family. One week away won't demolish your networking efforts. Because there really is no way to rush the networking process, build at least a few days "off the job" into each calendar quarter. Mark them on your planning calendar with a bright-colored marker and use them as a carrot-on-the-stick to keep you moving.

As part of the orchestration of your search, evaluate your finances and do some short-, medium- and long-term contingency planning. Don't let the uncertainty of the search process force you into draconian measures that make you and your family feel like deprived martyrs. Keep your overall life equation as stable as possible, for your own sanity and that of your spouse and children. Keep your networking efforts confined to a pace that you find comfortable, manageable and sustainable.

Pointless Networking

Over and above nurturing your existing network, build time into your business schedule to meet and cultivate still more contacts. For some people, this is in their nature. They love looking into other people's lives, learning new things, interacting, collaborating. They may not even be aware of how they're empowering themselves.

War Story: Where common sense comes from

A woman executive who is known far and wide for "having an enormous amount of common sense" seems singularly well-rooted, with a pragmatic turn of mind that serves her and her company well. Most people assume this strength is the result of some innate intellectual gift, some natural aptitude for seeing to the heart of things.

She's certainly endowed with good critical thinking powers, but much of what others are so quick to label common sense derives from a phenomenal supply of anecdotal information. She simply knows a lot about a lot of things and a lot of people. Her knowledge goes deeper than the formal version of reality printed in newspapers and press releases. She always seems to know "what's really happening" behind the scenes. Few topics come up on which she can't add some practical insight based on having a richer source of information than the other participants in the conversation.

Where does she get this font of uncommon knowledge that others call "common sense"? She engages in "pointless networking"—lunches, breakfasts and meetings that have no perceptible agenda. If she reads about a person whom she finds interesting, she introduces herself, suggests they get acquainted, and usually acquires a friend (or at least a new source of information). She's not devious or manipulative; she's just curious. She finds different people interesting and seeks them out from a broad range of industries, levels and callings. She has never had to run a job search, so the thought that she's "networking" has never occurred to her. But she is:

- ☆ Gathering a lot of informal information;
- ☆ Acquiring enormous visibility along the way;
- ☆ Meeting a constant stream of new people.

That sure sounds like networking.

Just Do It

The Nike™ motto, "Just Do It!" must work, or the company wouldn't sell so many shoes. It appeals to people because it strikes a chord that resonates within most of us: at some point, all the planning, theorizing and preparation are through and it's time to cut to the chase. The longest journey begins with a single step, and so do the short journeys. You have to decide it's time to start, and you have to be prepared for an exploration even though its duration and destination can't be mapped in advance.

Skilled and productive networking isn't a matter of luck, unless you define luck as "hard work meeting up with opportunity." We see no point in wishing good luck to those who have worked through this book. Instead, we wish you the good things that effective networking requires: Good self-awareness. Good planning. Good discipline. Good interpersonal skills. Good curiosity. Good faith. Good stamina. Good determination. Good confidence. Good optimism.

Go for it.

Index

No matter where your career is headed, one source will point you in the right direction.

National Business Employment Weekly

Turn to us whether you're looking for a new position or to improve your present one. We'll not only provide you with hundreds of nationwide and regional job opportunities, we'll help you with expert career advice. From letter and resume writing for the job seeker to negotiating and networking strategies for the seasoned professional, National Business Employment Weekly is your source. So, no matter where your career is headed, make your next move toward success by picking up the National Business Employment Weekly at your newsstand. Or get the next 12 issues delivered for just $52 by calling toll-free...

800-535-4800

THE WALL STREET JOURNAL.
NATIONAL BUSINESS EMPLOYMENT WEEKLY

3GDX

Call toll-free 800-535-4800
or fill out this coupon and mail to:
National Business Employment Weekly
Box 9100, Dept. W, Springfield, MA 01101

❑ Yes! Please send me the next twelve issues, my
check or money order for $52 is enclosed.

_____
Name

_____
Address
_____

_____
City

_____
State   Zip

SPECIAL BONUS!

RECEIVE ONE FREE ISSUE!
NATIONAL BUSINESS EMPLOYMENT WEEKLY

No matter where your career is headed, the *National Business Employment Weekly* points you in the direction of career success. Whether you're looking for a new position or to improve your present one, you'll find hundreds of nationwide and regional job opportunities—highly paid executive, professional and technical positions—available now. Send in the coupon and receive one free issue and you'll agree that NBEW is the nation's number one job search publication.